THE CONTEMPORARY KEYBOARDIST™
STYLISTIC ETUDES
by
JOHN NOVELLO

This work is dedicated to all of my students who in their quest to understand and master contemporary keyboard styles have given me the incentive to research and write this work.

Project Manager: Tony Esposito
Photo by: Neal "Chaz" Bowie
MIDI Sound Engineer: David Kates
Music Engraved by: Steve Einbinder
All Etudes performed by John Novello

ISBN 978-0-634-01092-7

HAL•LEONARD®
CORPORATION
7777 W. BLUEMOUND RD. P.O. BOX 13819 MILWAUKEE, WI 53213

Visit Hal Leonard Online at
www.halleonard.com

Author's Preface

One of the most difficult transitions for a pianist or keyboardist to make during his studies is from mechanics - ear training, scales, arpeggios, chords, rhythm, licks, etc - to actual musicianship - the ability to really play what you hear and communicate! In other words at some point the process must become synergistic meaning that the sum of all the parts (ear training, technique, harmony, rhythm, improvisation, and repertoire) is greater than the whole. Although the process is conceived as gradual, there is a point when the student of music becomes a musician and can actually play, perform, or as said in the jazz world - BLOW! The ear (actually just another name for the Spiritual Being in charge) takes over and literally consumes all knowledge and experience and simply directs the entire playing mechanism and instrument - the result being music! There is no thinking at this point, just hearing, playing and communicating!

The advantage of short exercises and drills is that they quickly get the student doing the necessary fundamentals and are therefore indispensable. However, they have their limit and shortcomings in that even when practiced in a musical way which they should always be, they are not a song, not the real thing. An analogy might be that a boxer or martial artist must practice many drills such as jumping rope, running, hitting the heavy bag and speed bag and practicing combinations but at some point he must spar and eventually get in the ring for a real fight or he'll never be able to measure his progress. In music, sparring would be equivalent to etude practice. An etude is a short musical piece which has as its purpose some instructional training which could be in the form of composition, musical styles, or various musical fundamentals such as hand independence, octave passages, counterpoint, dynamics, difficult keys, etc whereas a regular musical composition, which admittedly may also include these parameters, does not usually have this as its purpose. In other words the actual fight is not a training session but an actual fight to see who is the victor whereas the sparring match is still somewhat instructional but extremely close to the real thing.

This is the purpose of any etude study and indeed the purpose of The Contemporary Keyboardist Stylistic Etudes. After having taught over 30,000 hours of one on one private instruction, the most rewarding moments I have ever had are those when a student actually plays real music that not only communicates to others but also to himself. Like, hey, did you hear what I just played! The path I use to get a student to this point is the following;

1. Mastering of the music fundamentals of ear training, technique, harmony, rhythm, and improvisation
2. The playing of enough diverse repertoire until #1 & #2 merge into musicianship.

Since today's contemporary styles however are not as well documented as past styles - baroque, classical, impressionism, 20th century, etc, the written repertoire is very lacking in quantity and authenticity. Most great musicians conquer # 2 above by listening to recordings and concerts and trying their best to duplicate what they hear with the talents they have. Some do quite well making this transition and others not so well. So I got the idea that wouldn't it be nice if there were many short songs (etudes) that not only contained various fundamentals but also taught authentically many of the various contemporary commercial styles. Look as I did, I couldn't find any. Most of the books I came across were either in the hot lick or short exercise format or arranged versions of hit songs and to be frank, not at all authentic - meaning not the "blowing" you hear on the real recordings. So the challenge was to write many short songs or etudes that a) accurately conveyed the various contemporary musical styles - blues, jazz, fusion, rock, pop, reggae, gospel, country, new age, etc but not make them b) too long and c) too difficult and d) still have them contain key musical fundamentals. The result is The Contemporary Keyboardist Stylistic Etudes. Hope you like them!

Good luck,

John Novello

Introduction

Welcome to the Contemporary Keyboardist Stylistic Etudes. Etude is French for "study" which means in this case a song that also teaches some style and/or musicianship fundamental. In this volume there are 86 etudes covering a wide range of contemporary styles and music fundamentals. Each etude comes with a score and a brief summary. The score includes chord changes and suggested fingerings as well. The summaries instruct you as to the style, the fundamentals covered, and my personal suggestions. You should listen first to the recording and then begin your practice which should include the following steps for maximum benefit;

1. Hands separately slowly and then gradiently faster up to tempo
2. Hands together slowly and then gradiently faster up to tempo
3. Transpose your favorite etudes to all keys for maximum results
4. Use these etudes as food for thought and thus
    a. Improvise on them as to interpretation, dynamics, melody, harmony, and rhythm.
    b. Find applications for them in your personal playing
    c. Write your own etudes as may be necessary.

It has been my experience that one of the hardest bridges for a musician to cross is the one from mechanics - theory, exercises, etc - to real musicianship and professional playing. I hope these studies assist you in this endeavor

And remember, if it isn't fun, it isn't music.

Go for it!

•

How To Use These Etudes

To All teachers and Students

This work is intended for the advanced beginner to intermediate. A certain level of ability is assumed in the areas of ear training, technique, harmony, and rhythm. Each etude is analyzed as to its style and as to what musical fundamentals are covered. Depending on your level and your interest, you can pick the appropriate etudes in the order you wish. For best results, each etude should be learned up to tempo and practiced in all keys. For those who have already had instruction in improvisation, each etude should be improvised on as well as in reality, they are only meant to be food for thought. I have included a recording(available in cassette, CD or MIDI File) as a guide to the intended stylistic sound. You should try playing along with the recording once you have mastered it. Feel free however to experiment yourself at different tempos and interpretations.

Besides being an excellent source as to playing contemporary styles, these etudes will also give you an insight into composing in these styles. You should try composing your own etudes for only then will you really master the fundamentals necessary to great musicianship.

John Novello

4

Contents

Contents Continued

CD Track Index

CD Track

CD Track Index Continued

CD Track

ETUDE #1

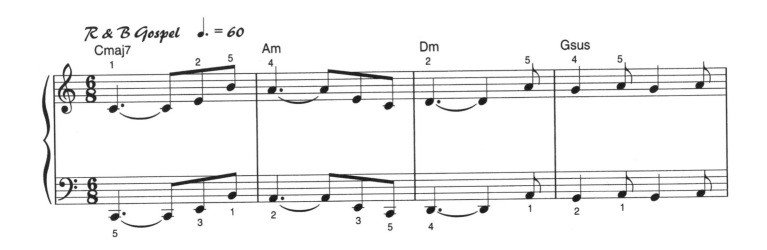

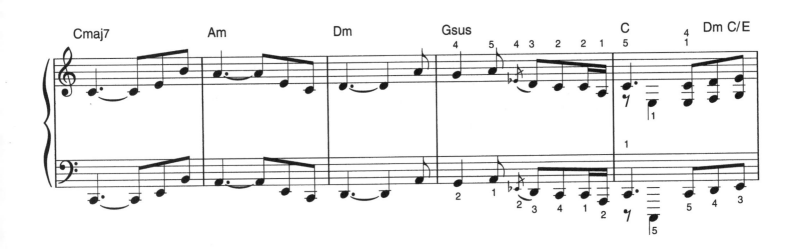

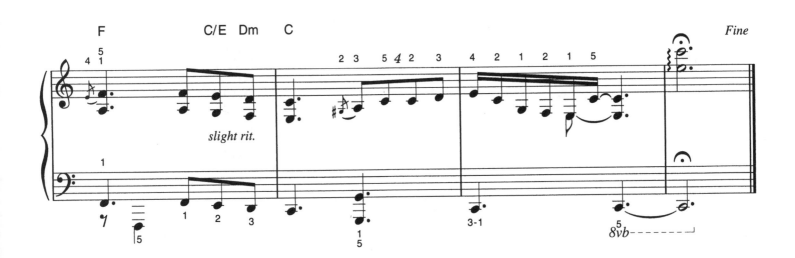

ETUDE #2

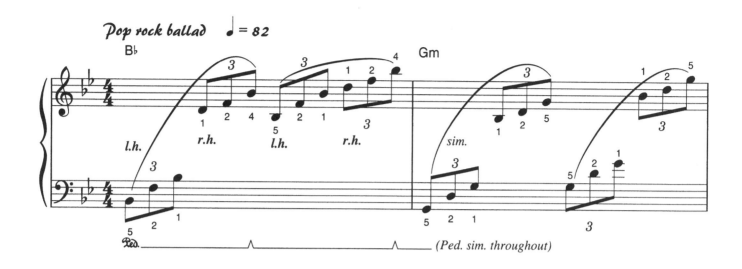

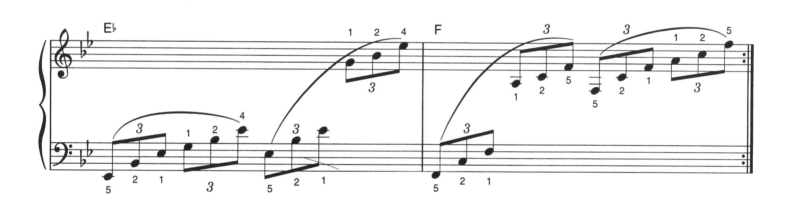

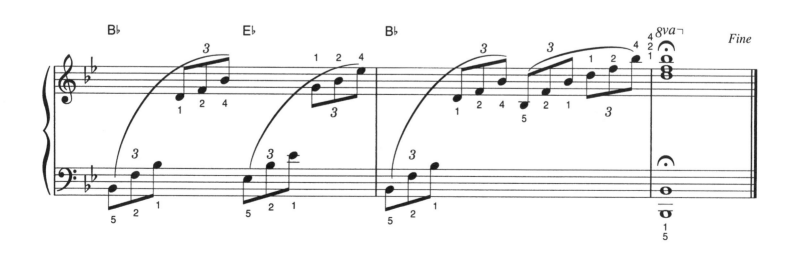

ETUDE #3

Pop ballad
Slowly, with expression

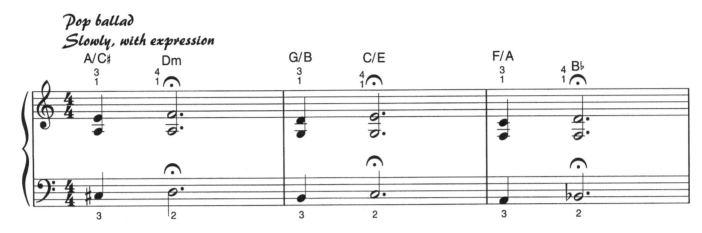

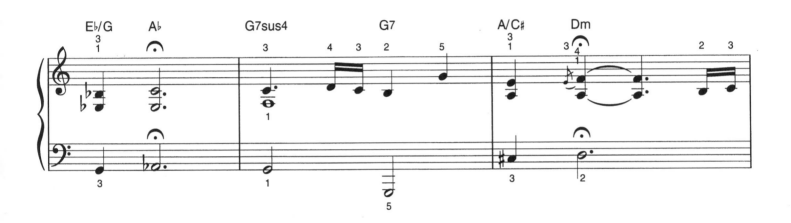

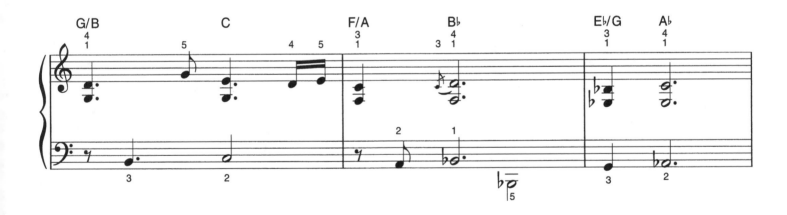

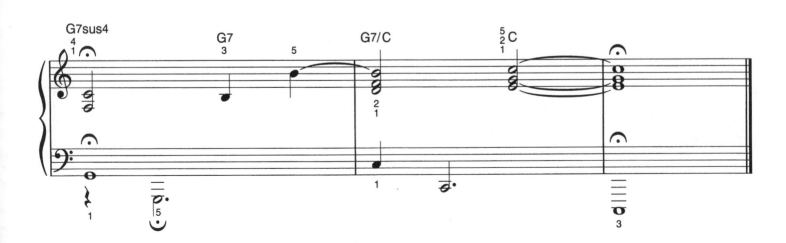

ETUDE #4

ETUDE #5

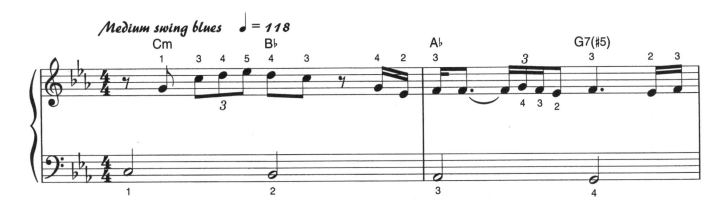

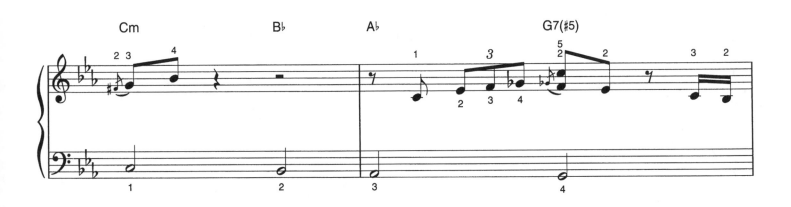

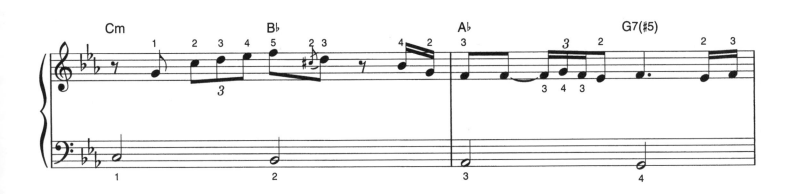

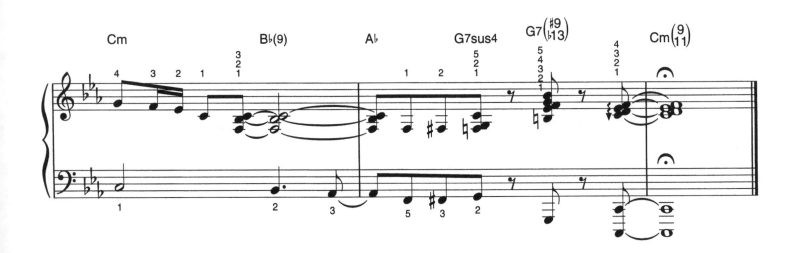

ETUDE #6

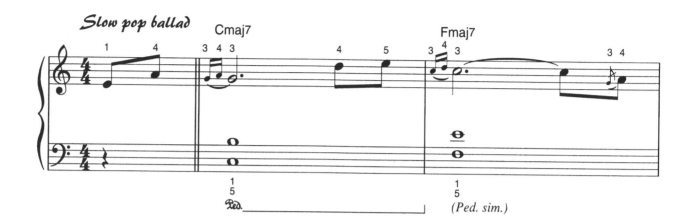

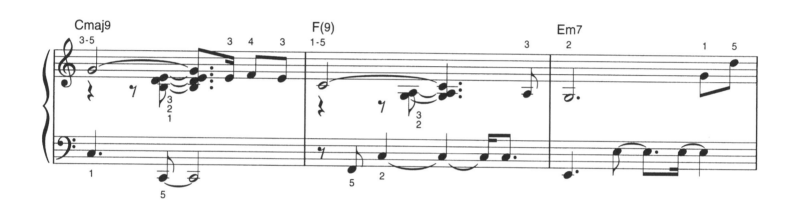

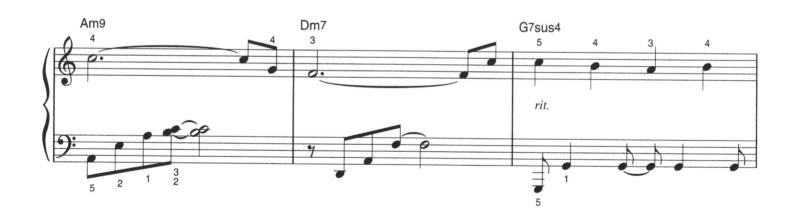

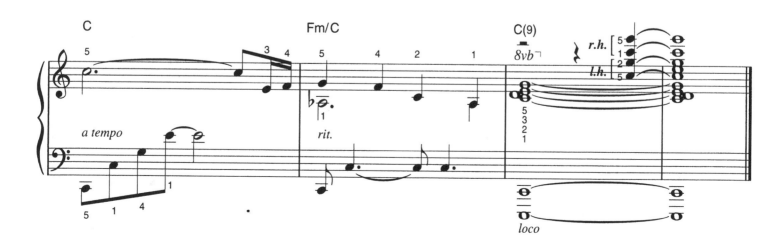

ETUDE #7

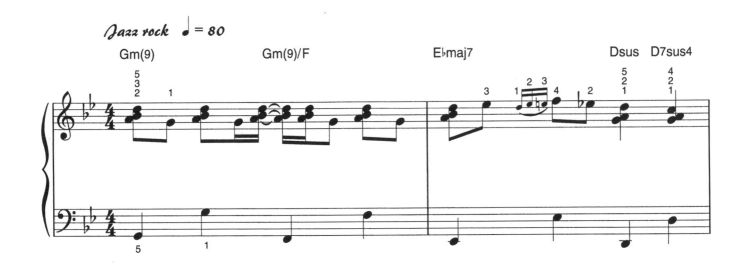

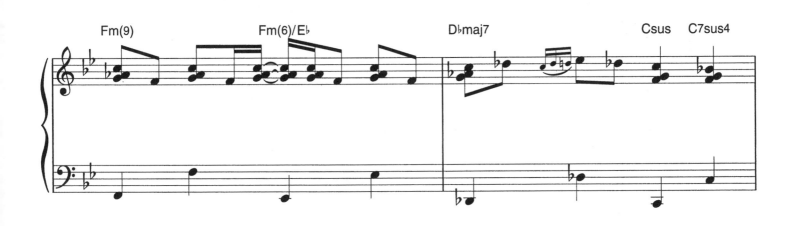

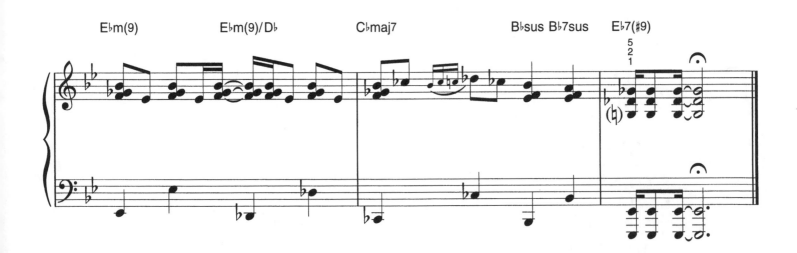

ETUDE #8

ETUDE #9

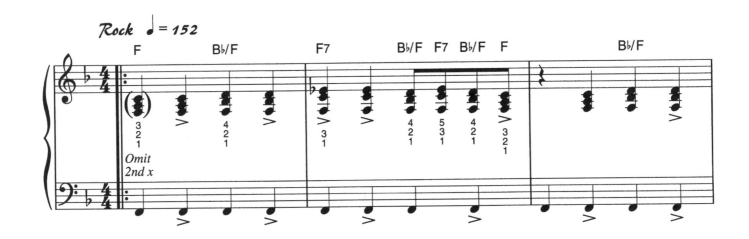

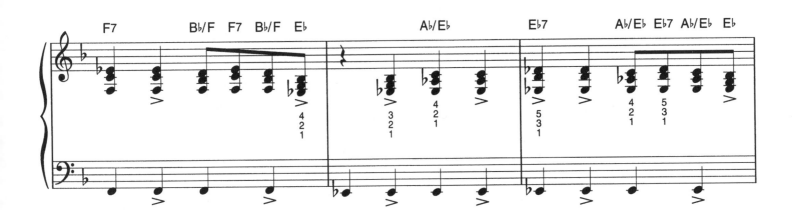

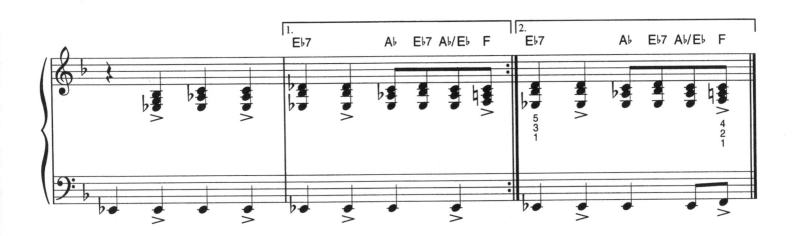

ETUDE #10

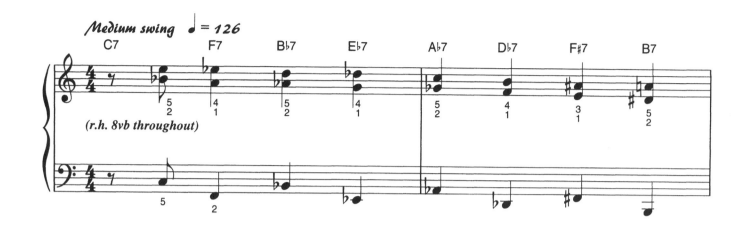

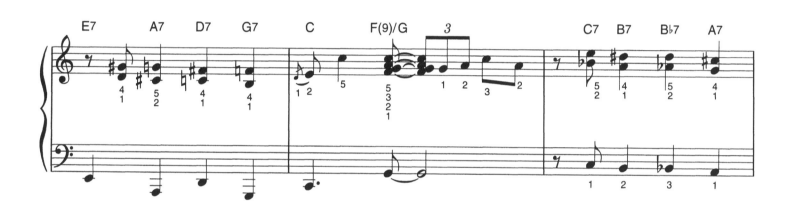

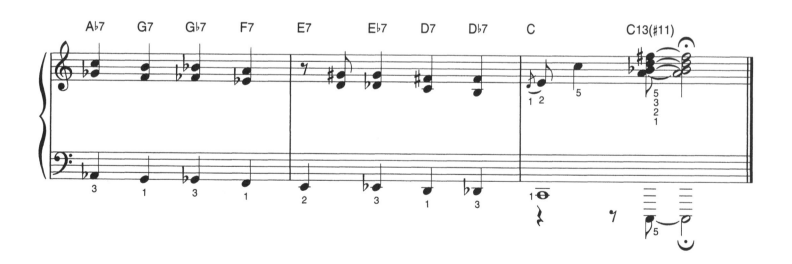

ETUDE #11

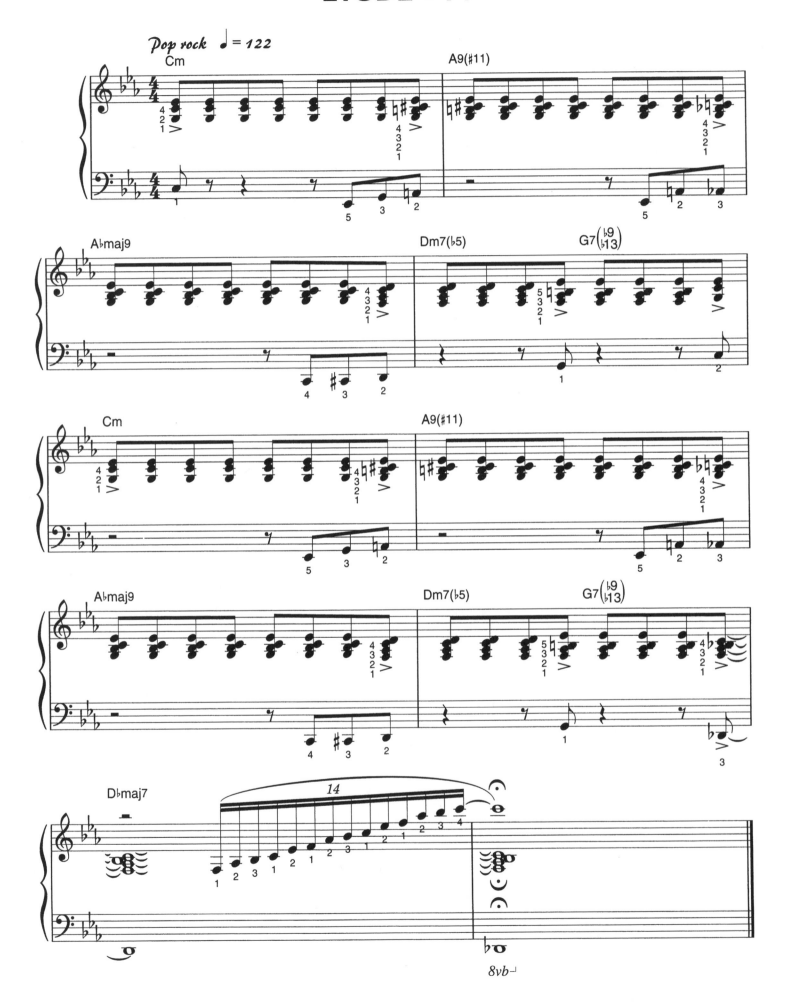

ETUDE #12

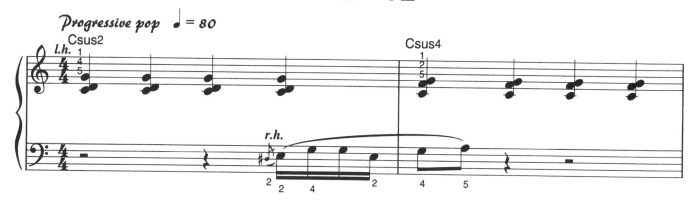

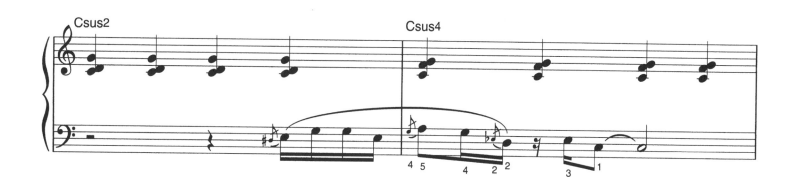

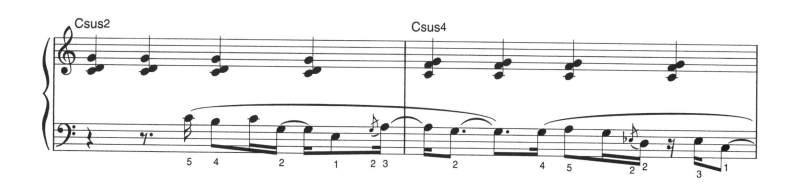

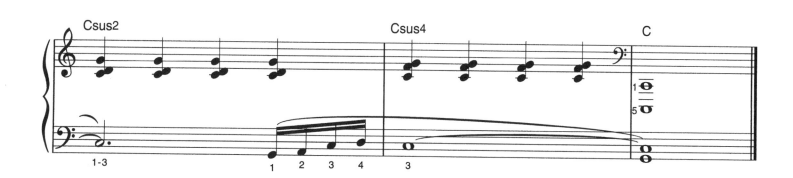

ETUDE #13

New Age Jazz Ballad

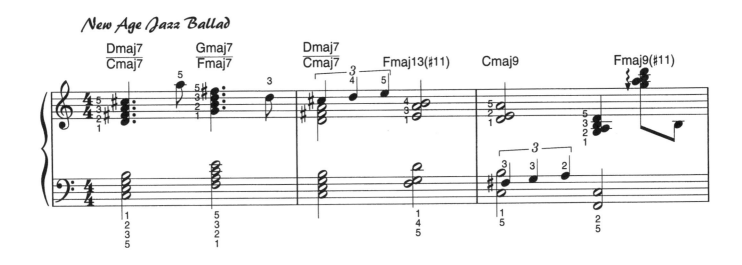

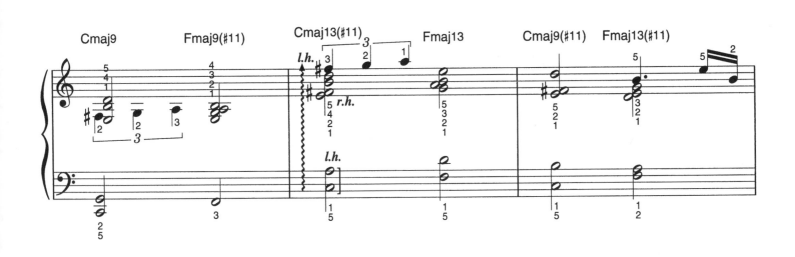

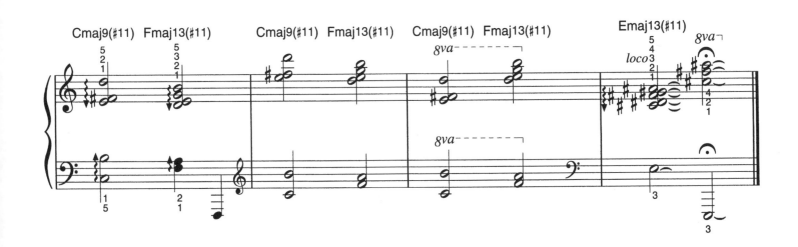

ETUDE #14

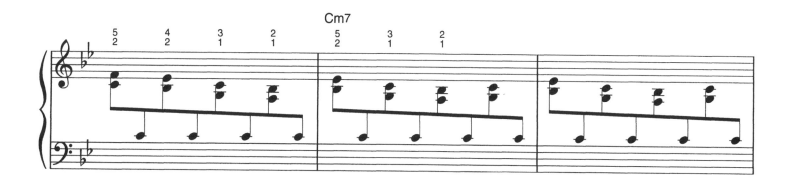

ETUDE #15

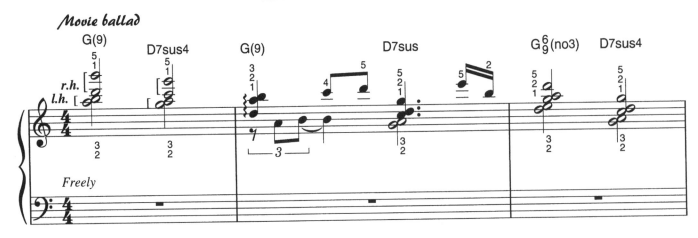

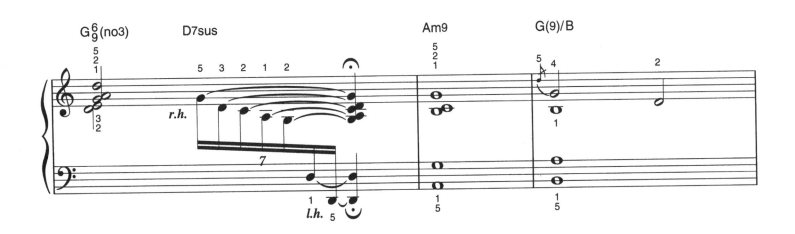

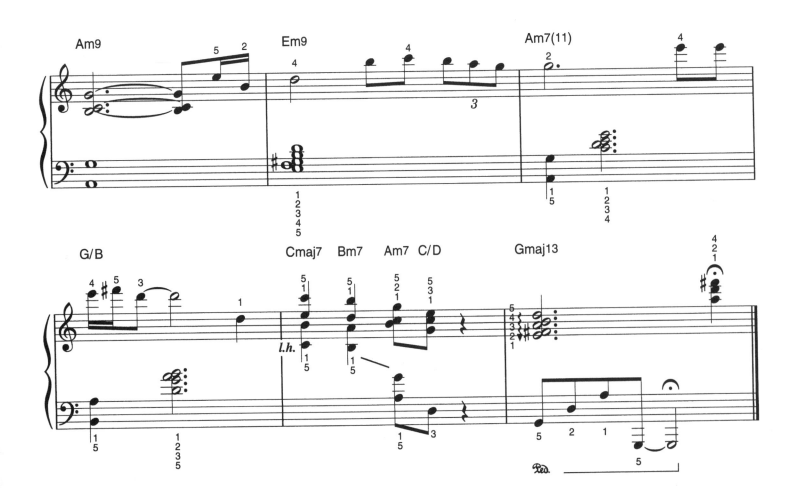

ETUDE #16

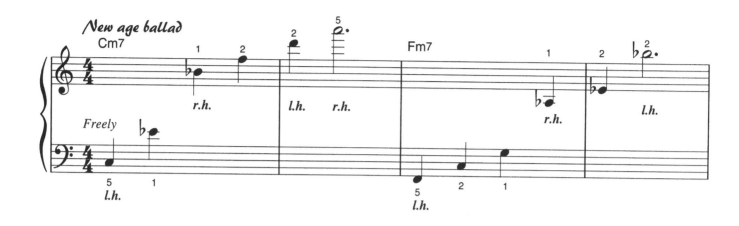

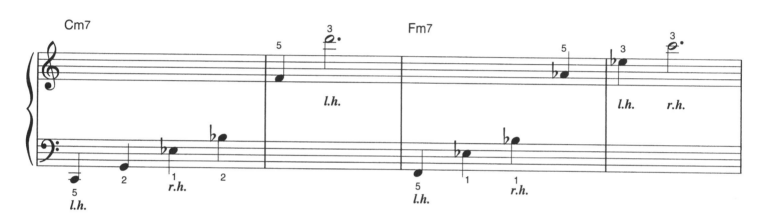

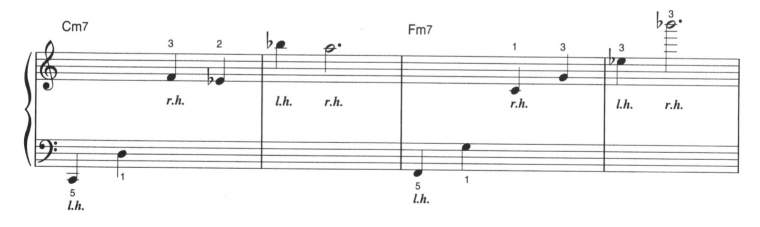

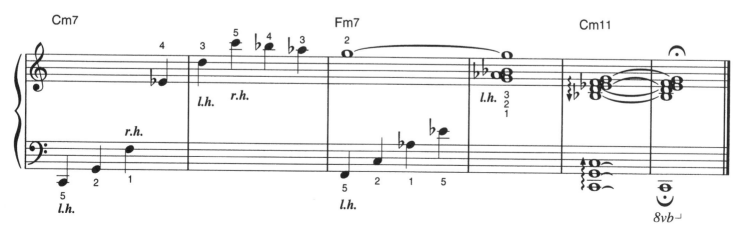

ETUDE #17

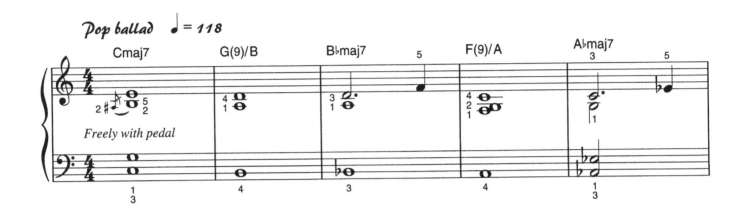

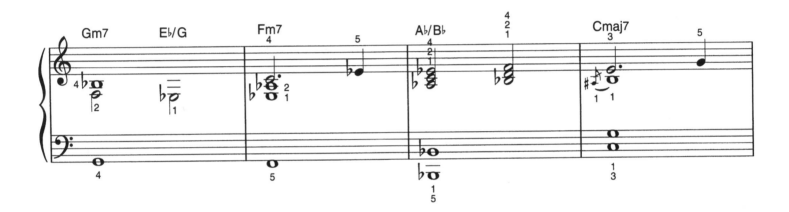

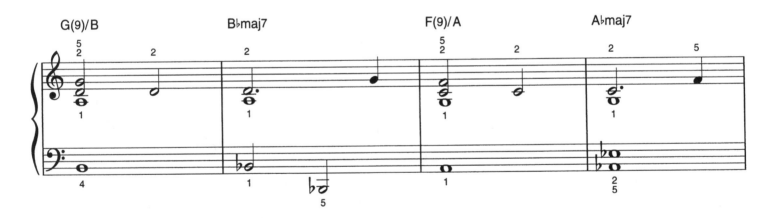

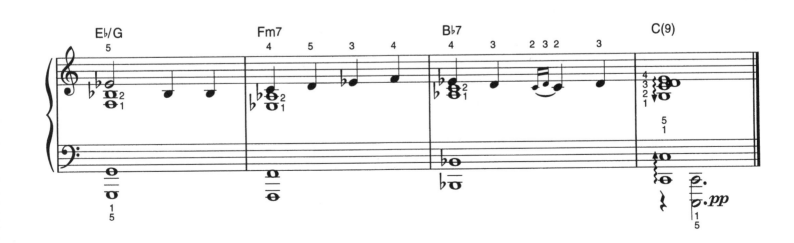

ETUDE #18

ETUDE #19

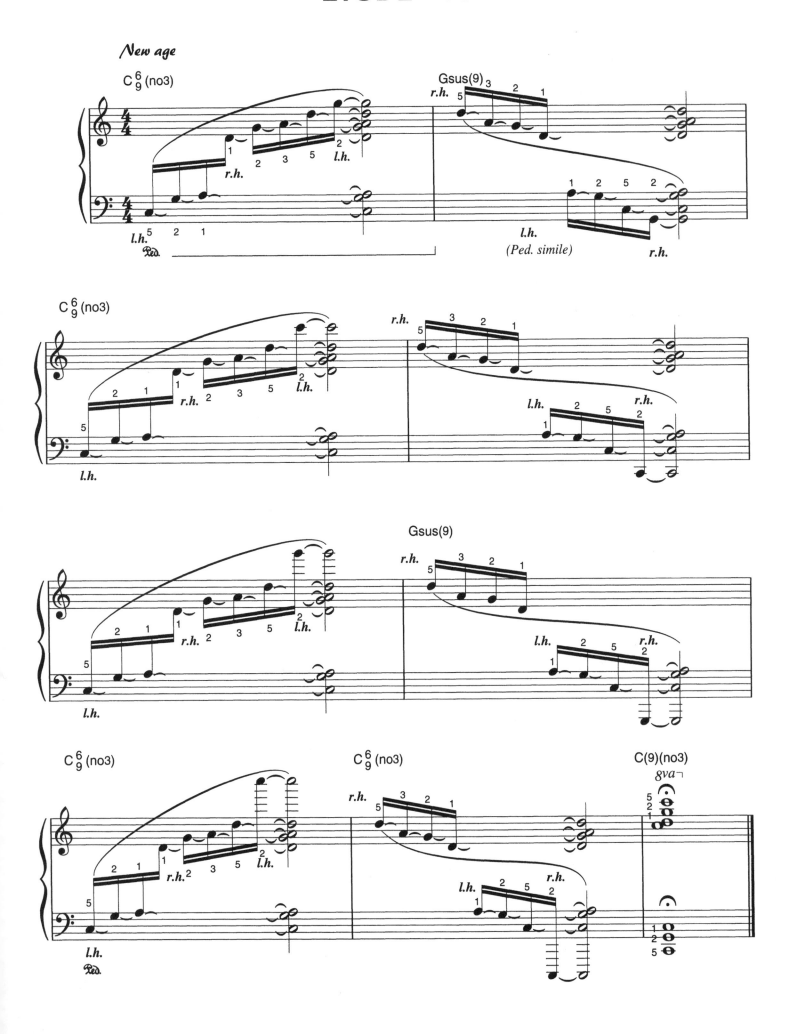

ETUDE #20

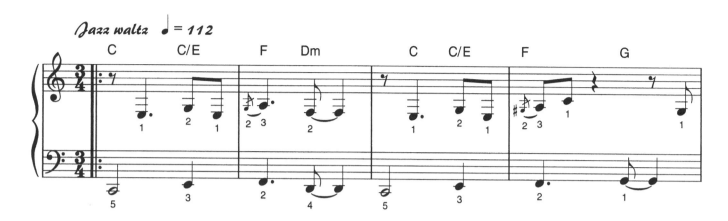

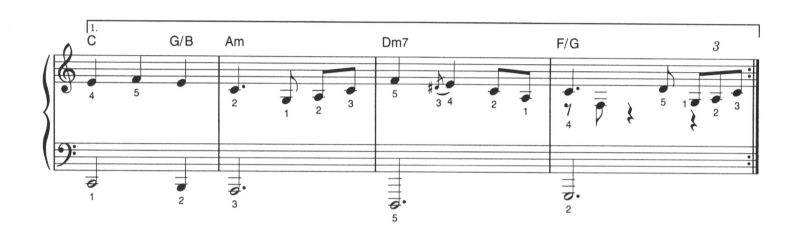

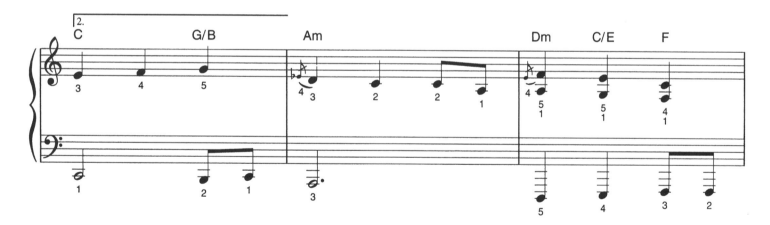

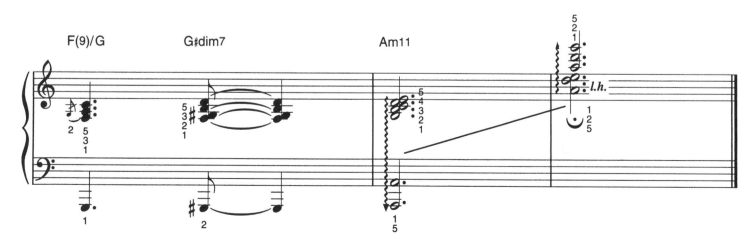

ETUDE #21

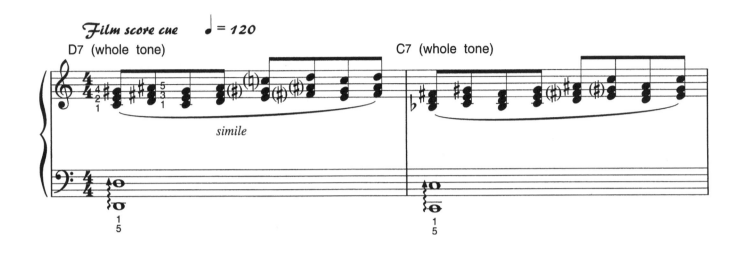

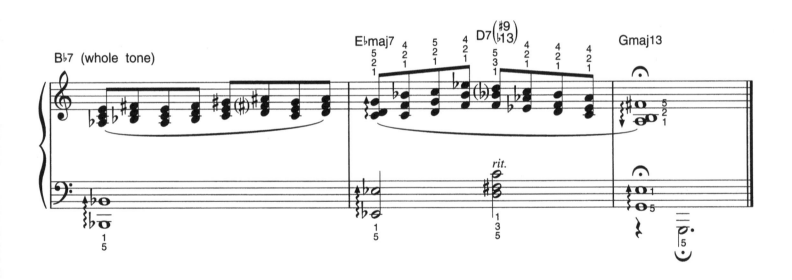

ETUDE #22

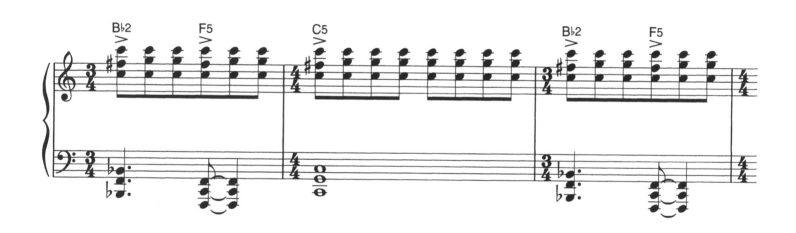

ETUDE #23

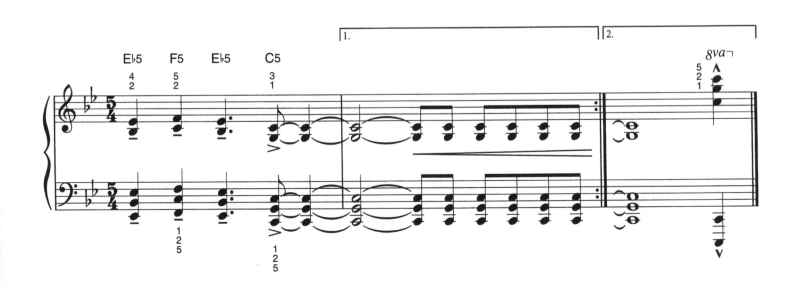

ETUDE #24

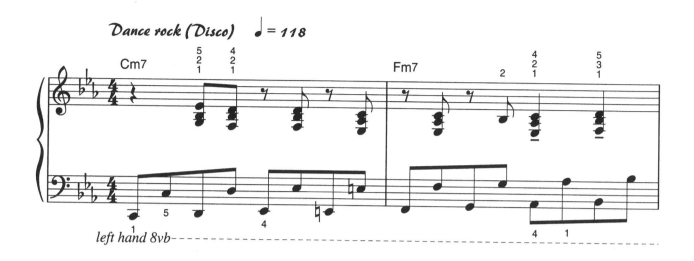

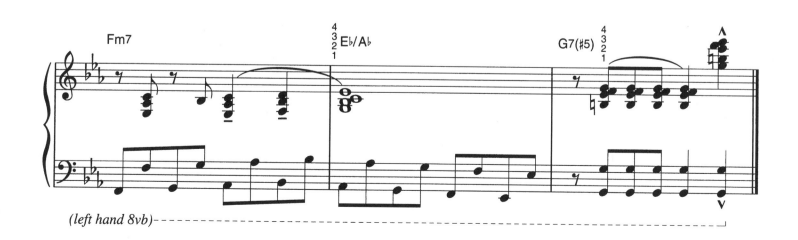

ETUDE #25

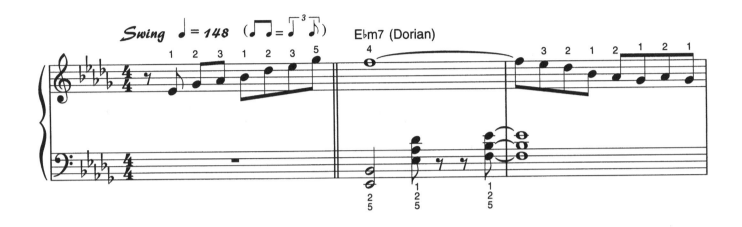

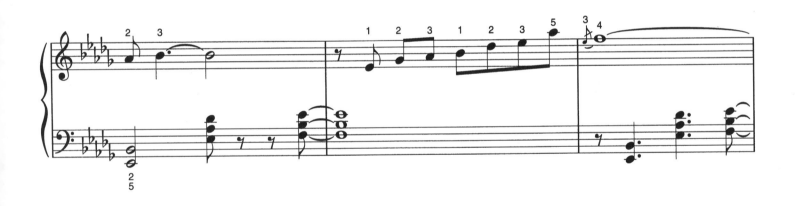

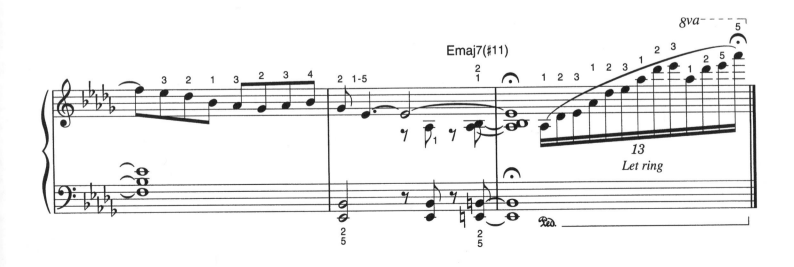

ETUDE #26

ETUDE #27

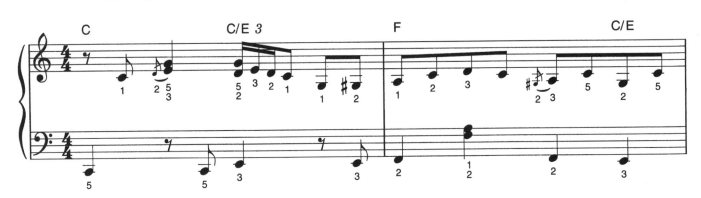

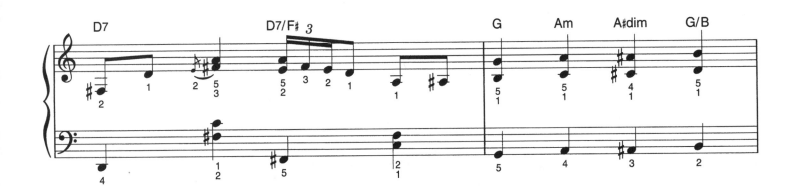

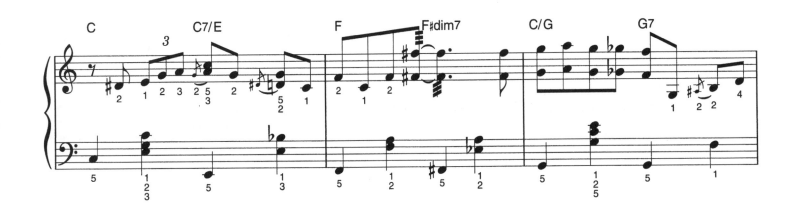

ETUDE #28

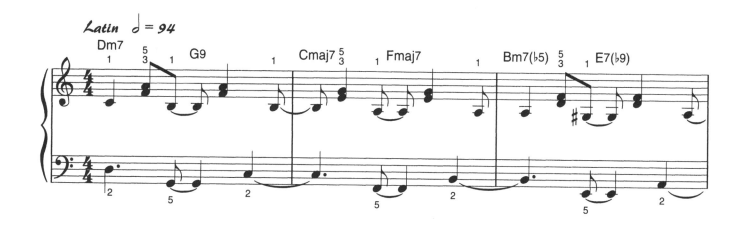

Repeat ad lib. and fade

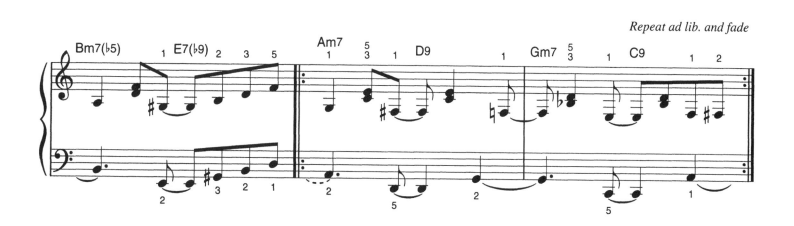

ETUDE #29

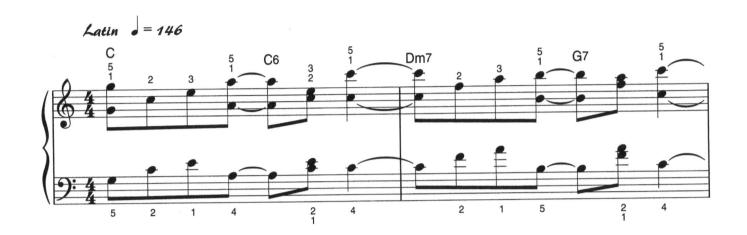

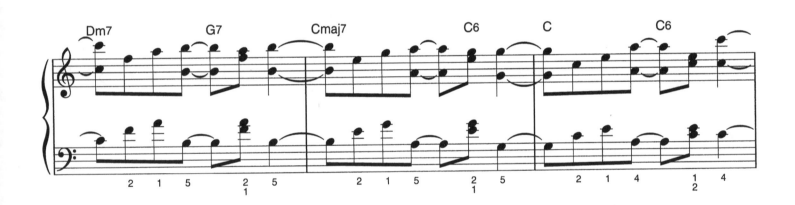

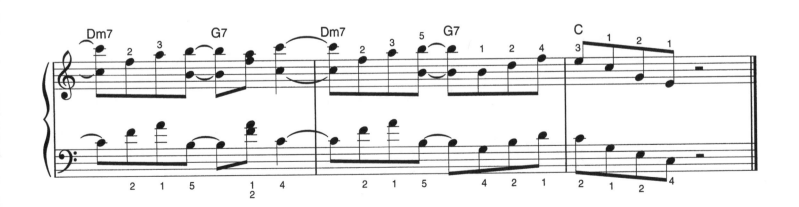

ETUDE #30

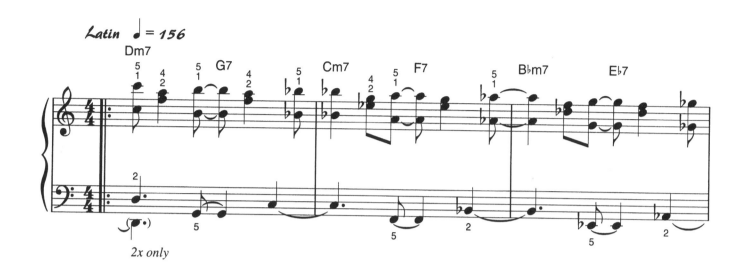

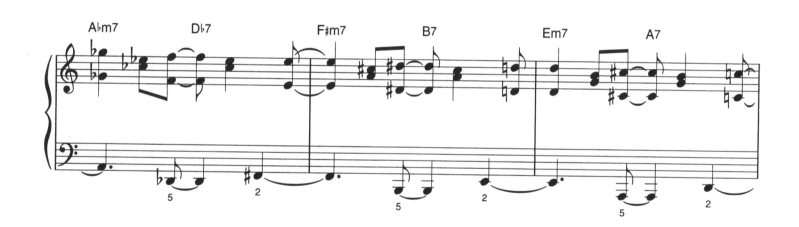

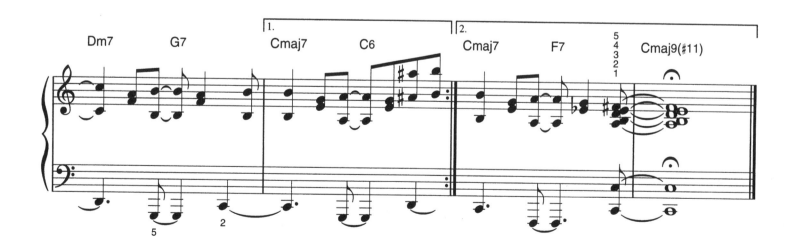

ETUDE #31

ETUDE #32

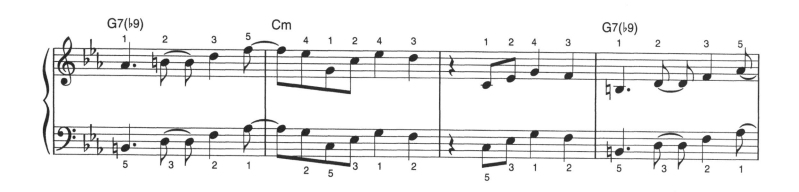

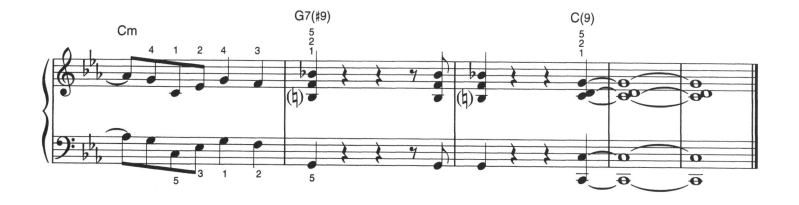

ETUDE #33

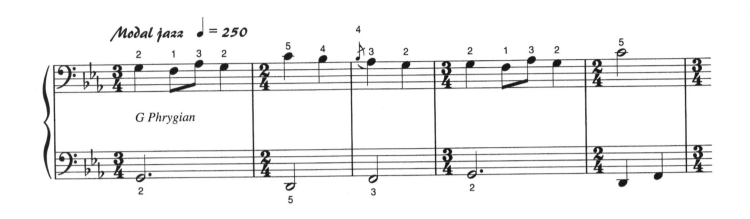

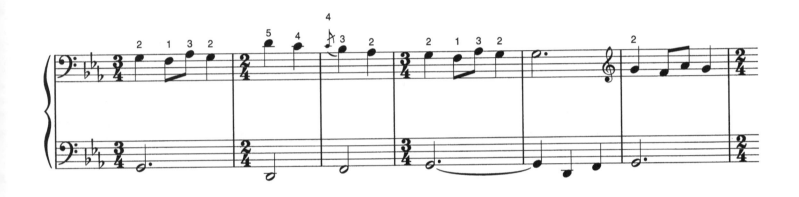

ETUDE #34

ETUDE #35

ETUDE #36

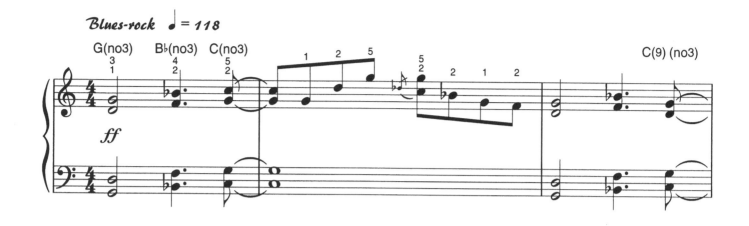

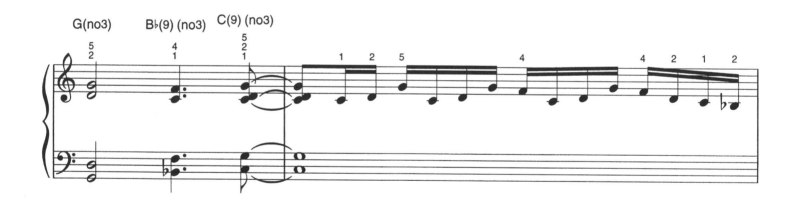

ETUDE #37

ETUDE #38

ETUDE #39

ETUDE #40

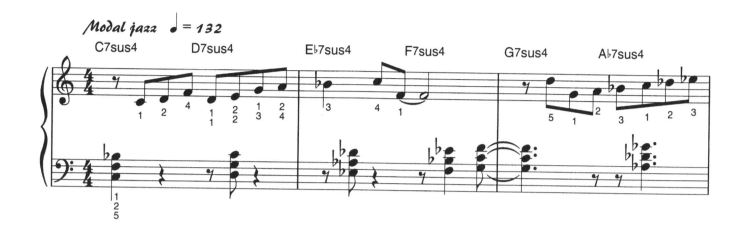

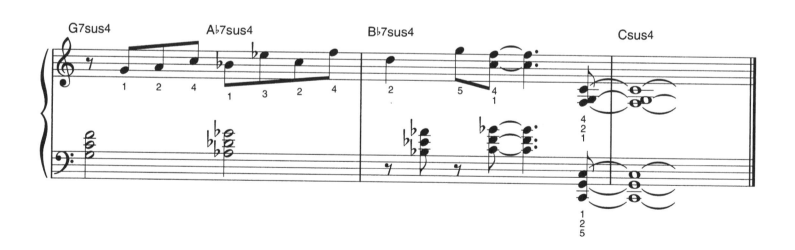

ETUDE #41

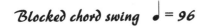

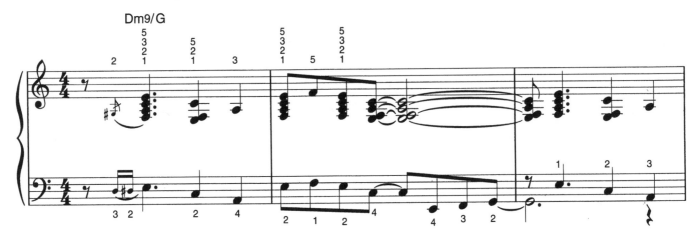

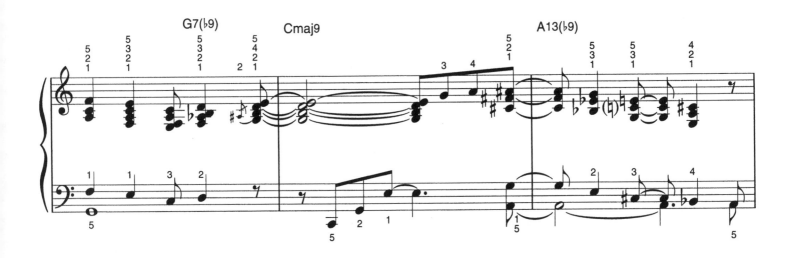

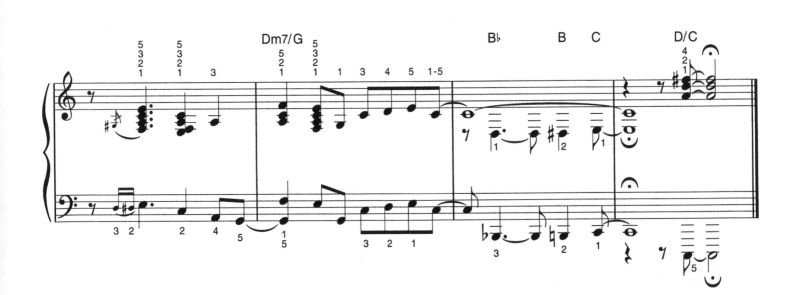

ETUDE #42

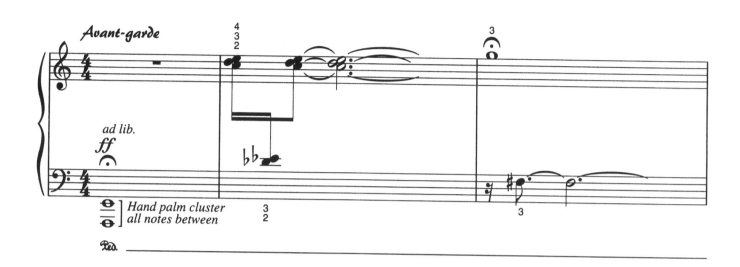

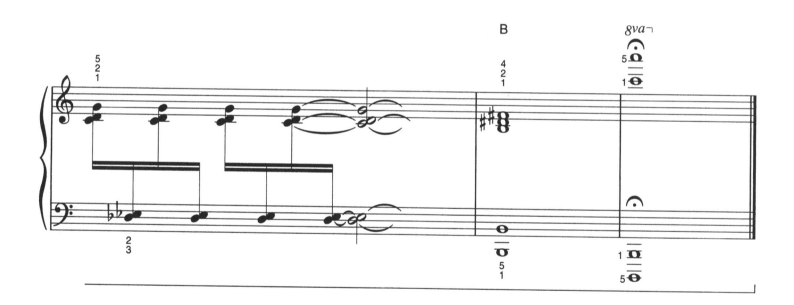

ETUDE #43

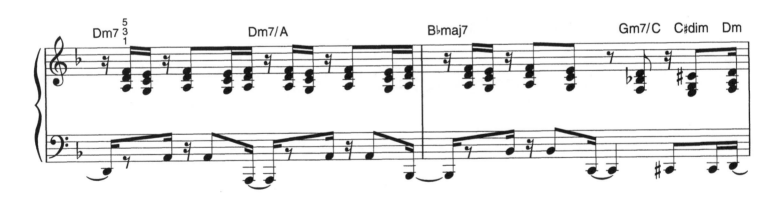

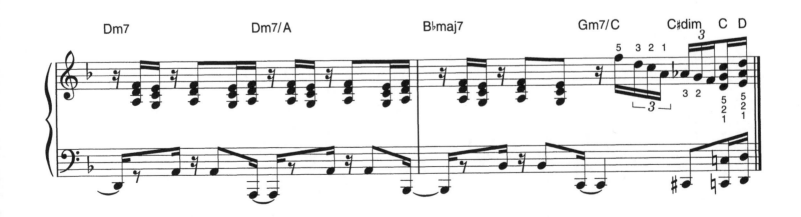

ETUDE #44

ETUDE #45

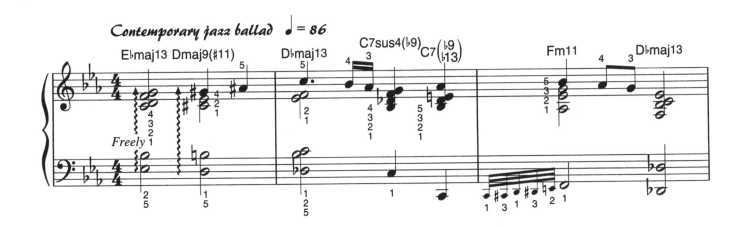

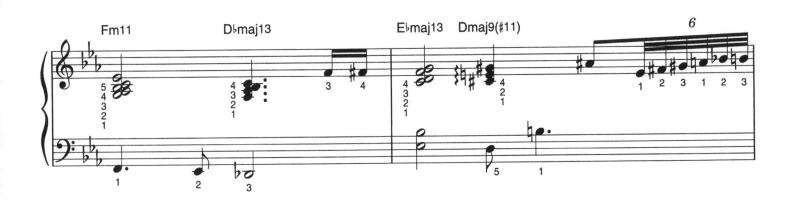

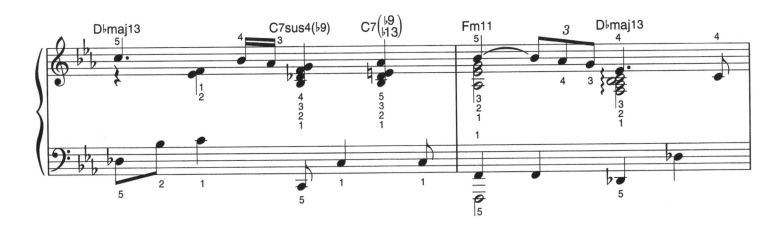

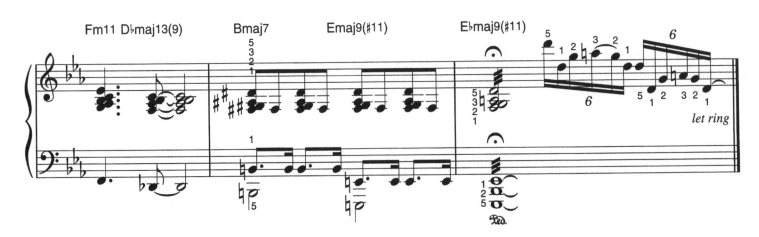

ETUDE #46

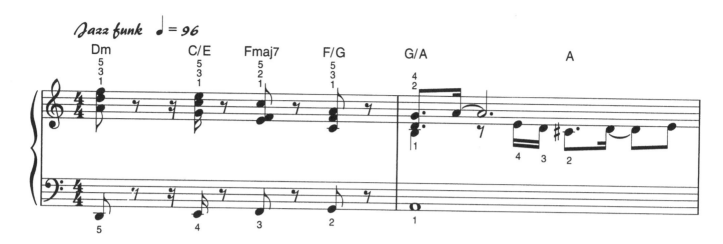

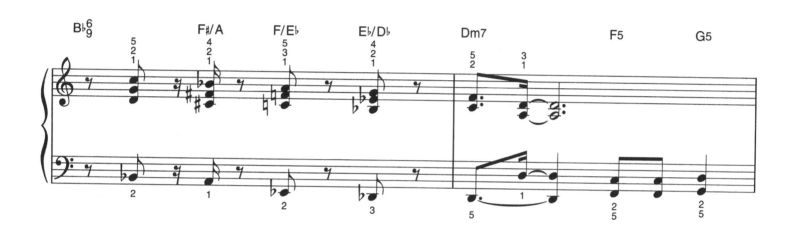

ETUDE #47

ETUDE #48

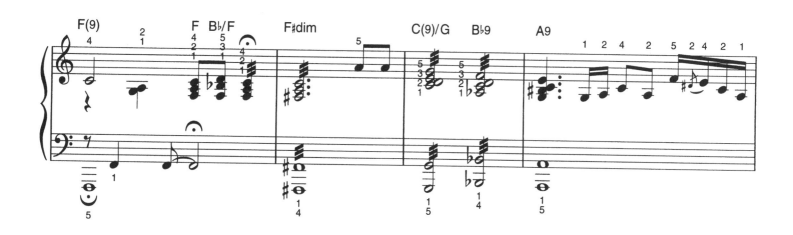

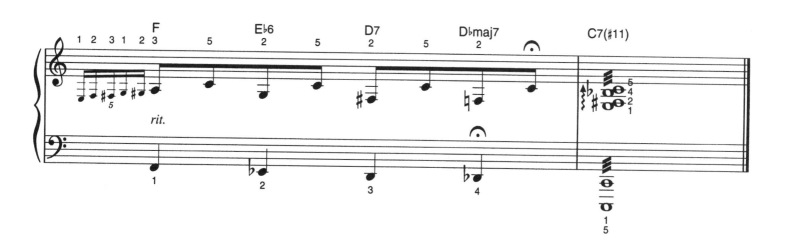

ETUDE #49

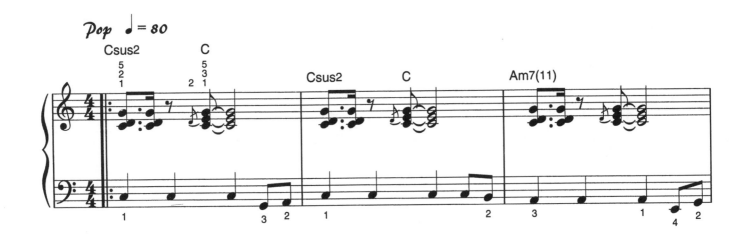

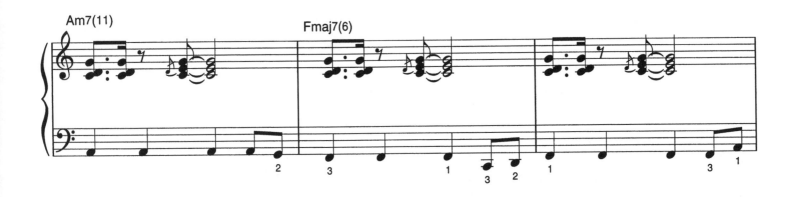

ETUDE #50

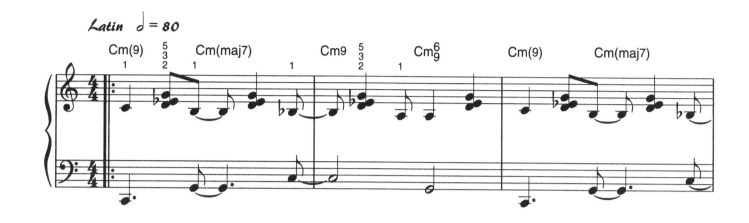

ETUDE #51

ETUDE #52

ETUDE #53

ETUDE #54

ETUDE #55

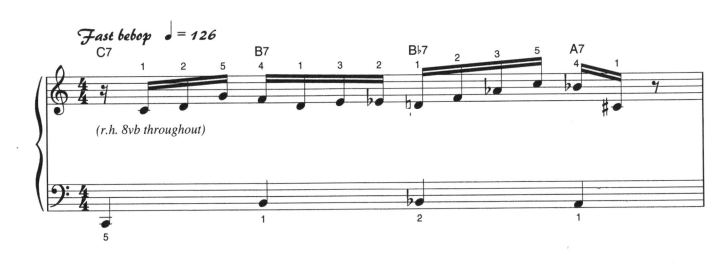

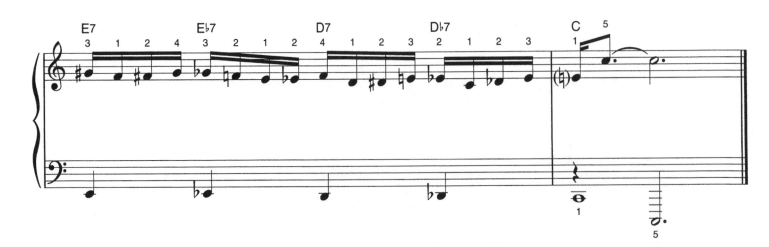

ETUDE #56

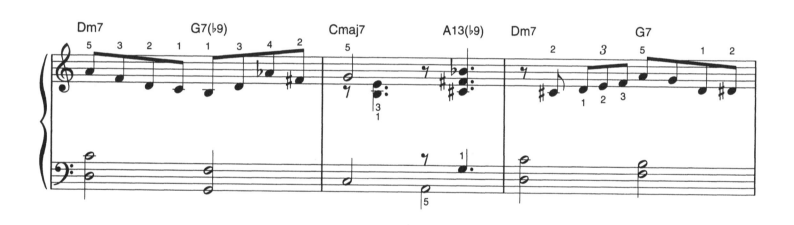

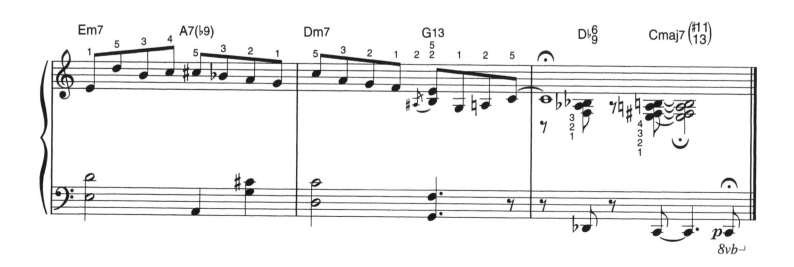

8vb

ETUDE #57

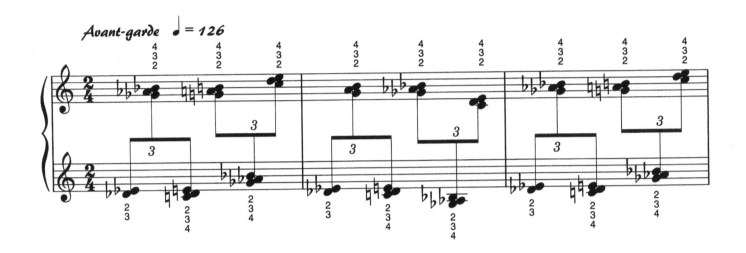

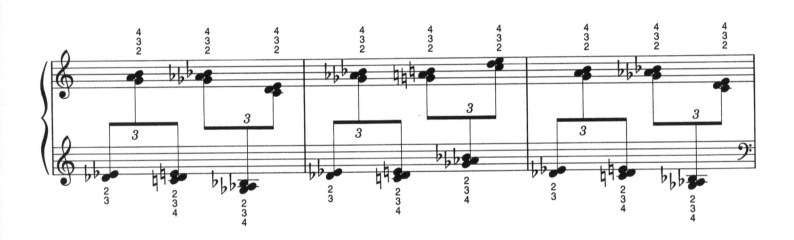

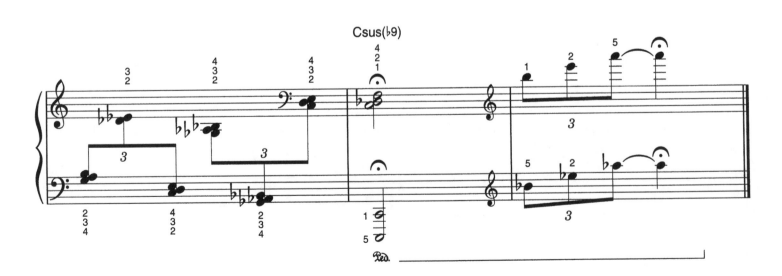

ETUDE #58

Classical pop

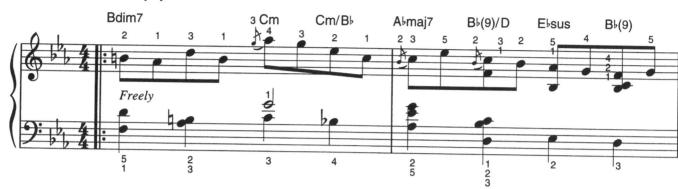

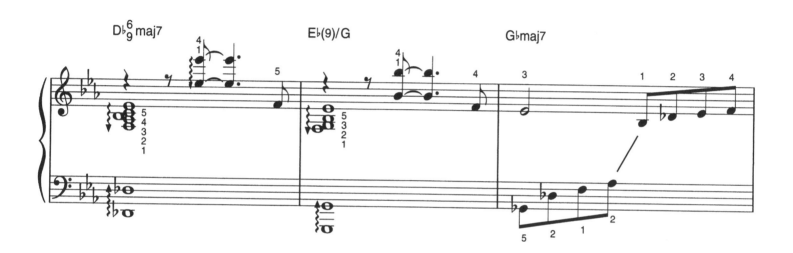

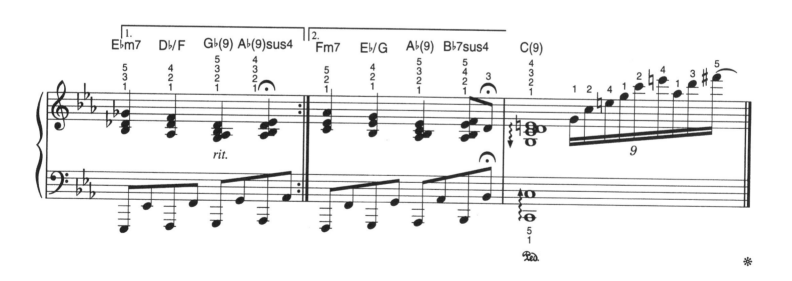

ETUDE #59

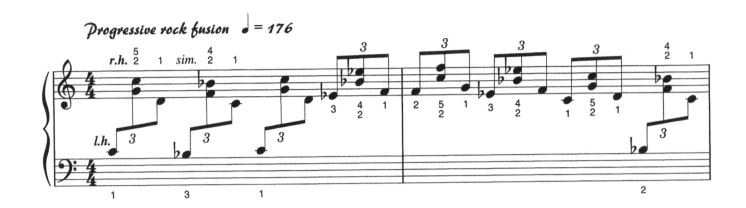

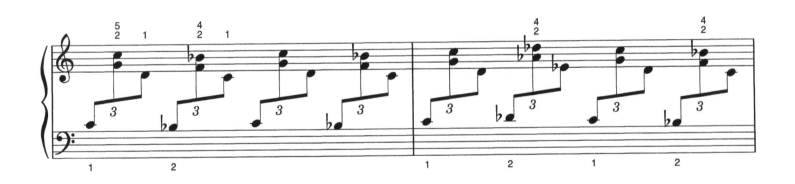

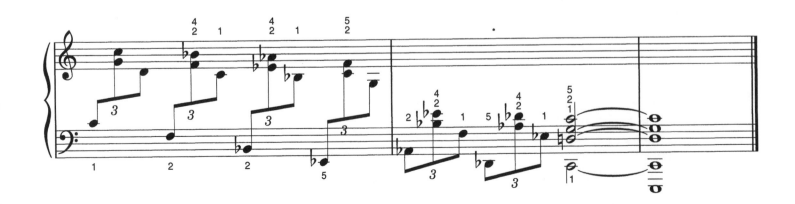

ETUDE #60

ETUDE #61

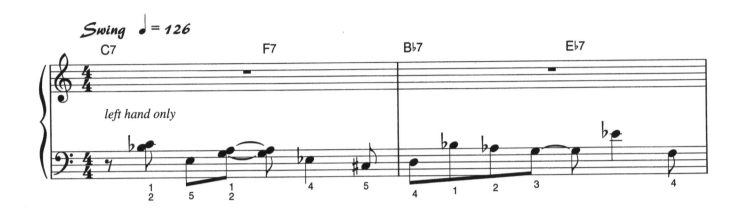

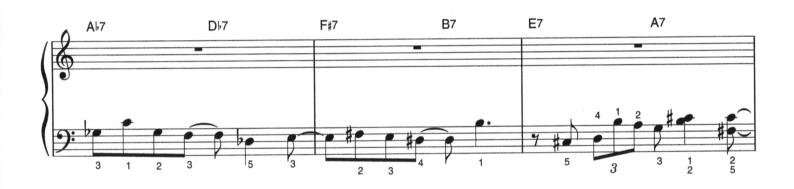

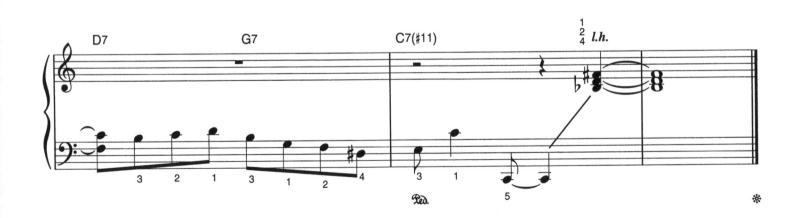

ETUDE #62

ETUDE #63

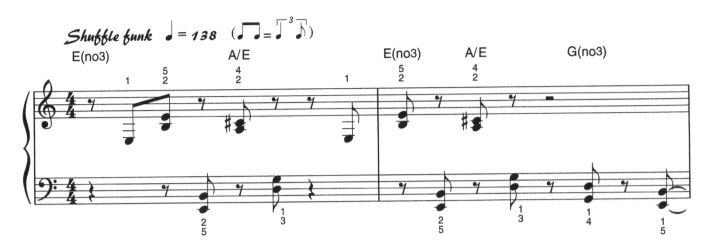

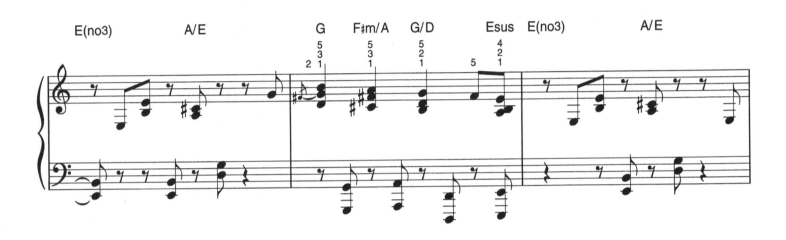

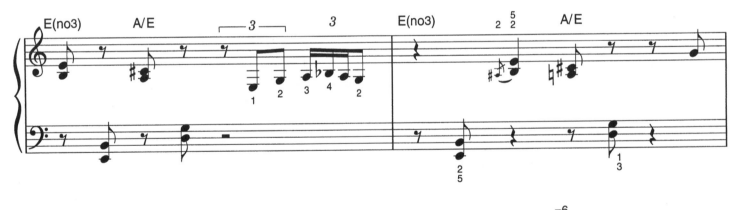

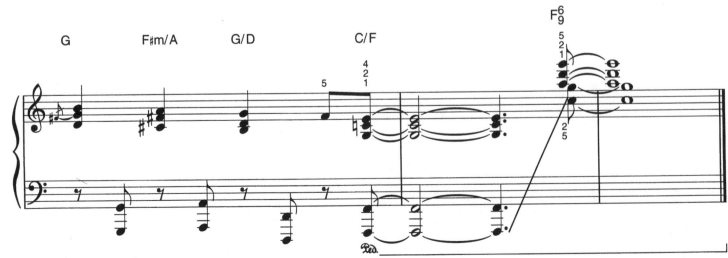

ETUDE #64

ETUDE #65

ETUDE #66

Chicago rock ♩ = 94

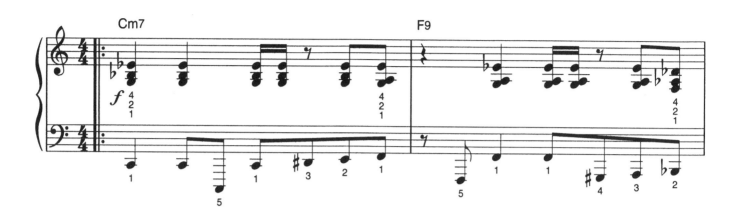

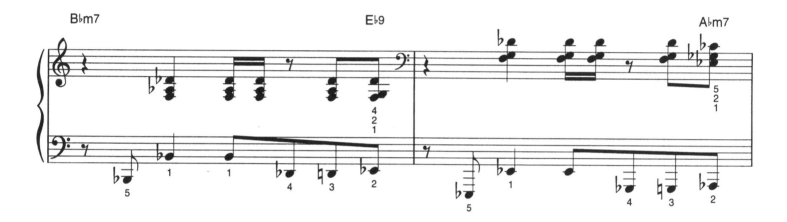

ETUDE #67

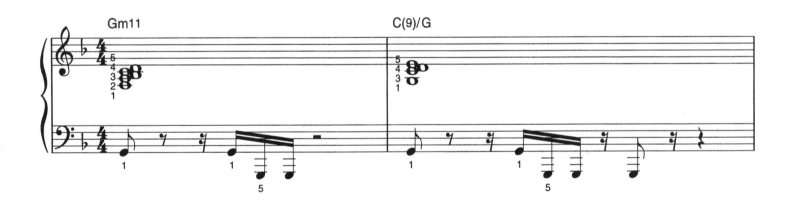

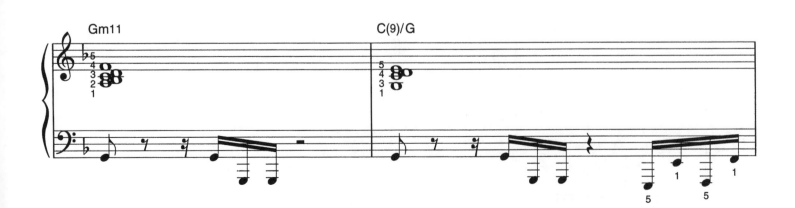

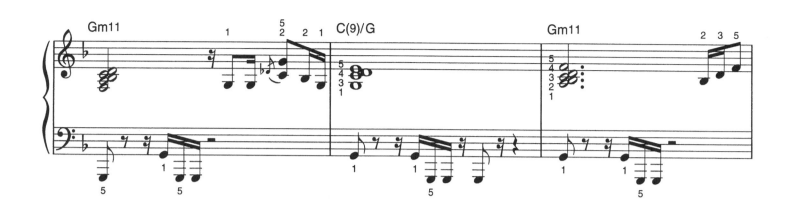

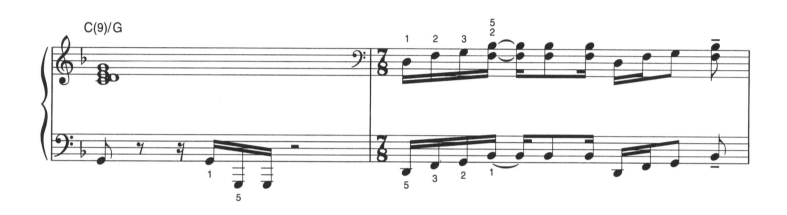

ETUDE #68

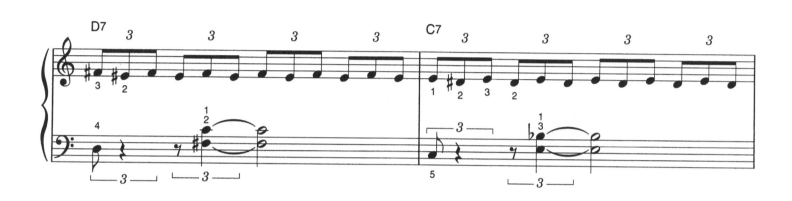

ETUDE #69

ETUDE #70

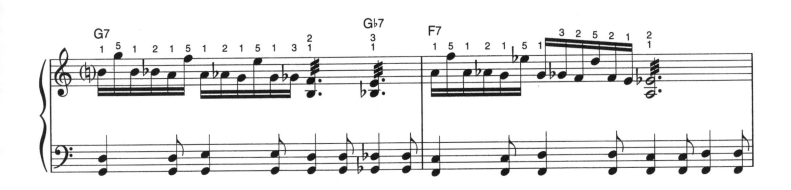

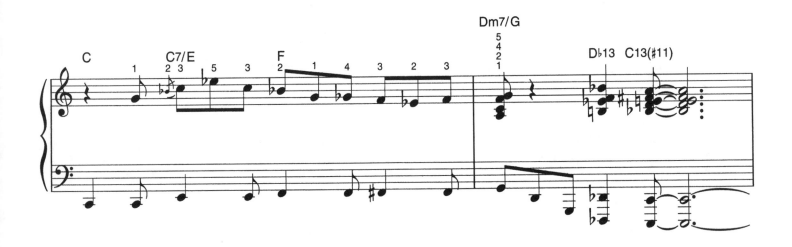

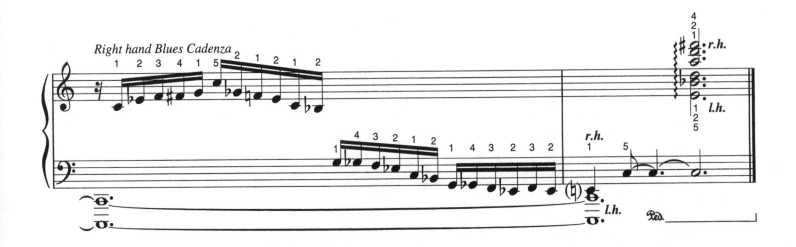

ETUDE #71

ETUDE #72

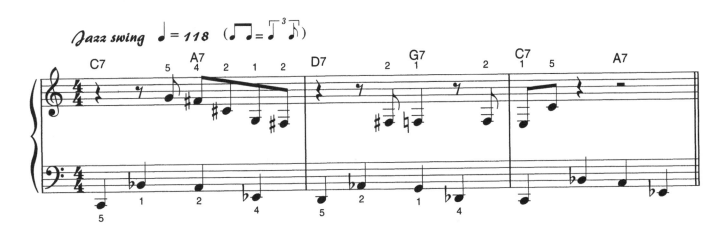

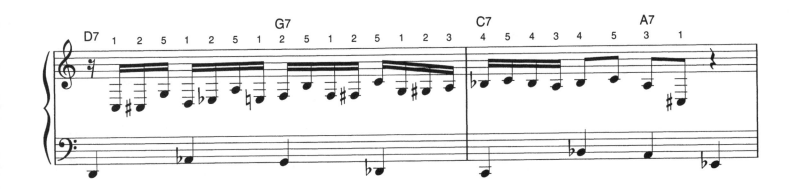

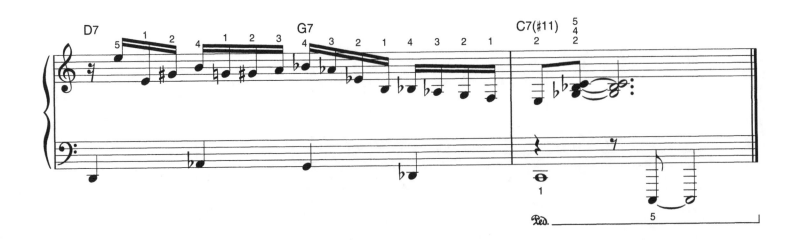

ETUDE #73

ETUDE #74

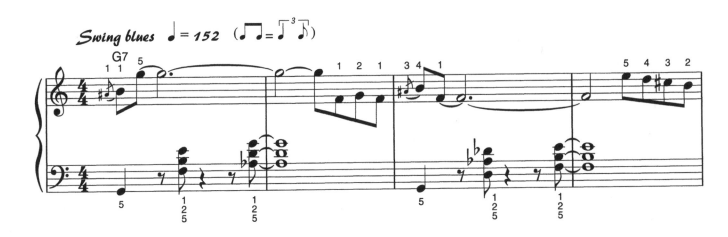

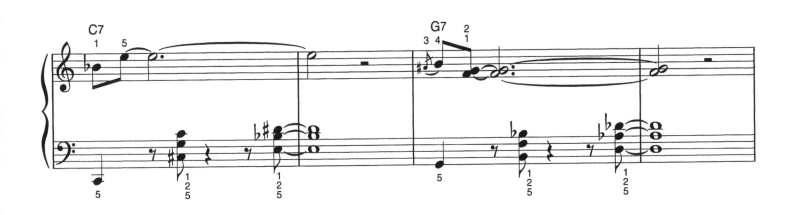

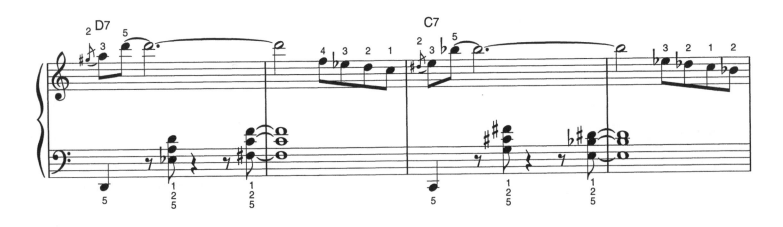

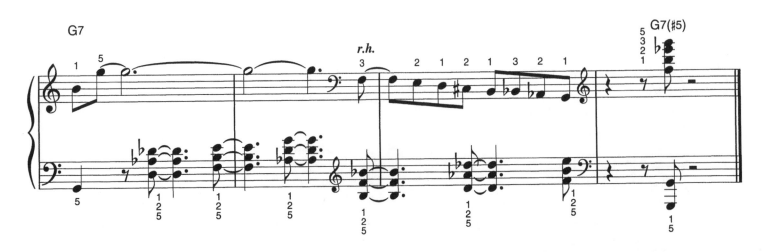

ETUDE #75

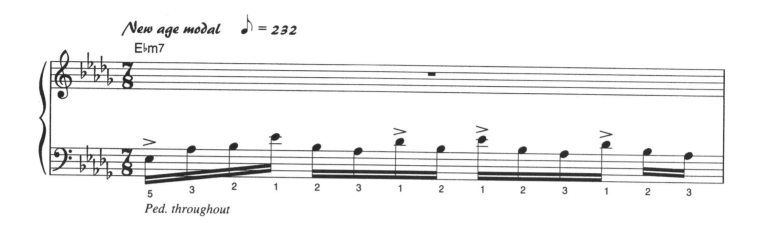

ETUDE #76

ETUDE #77

ETUDE #78

ETUDE #79

ETUDE #80

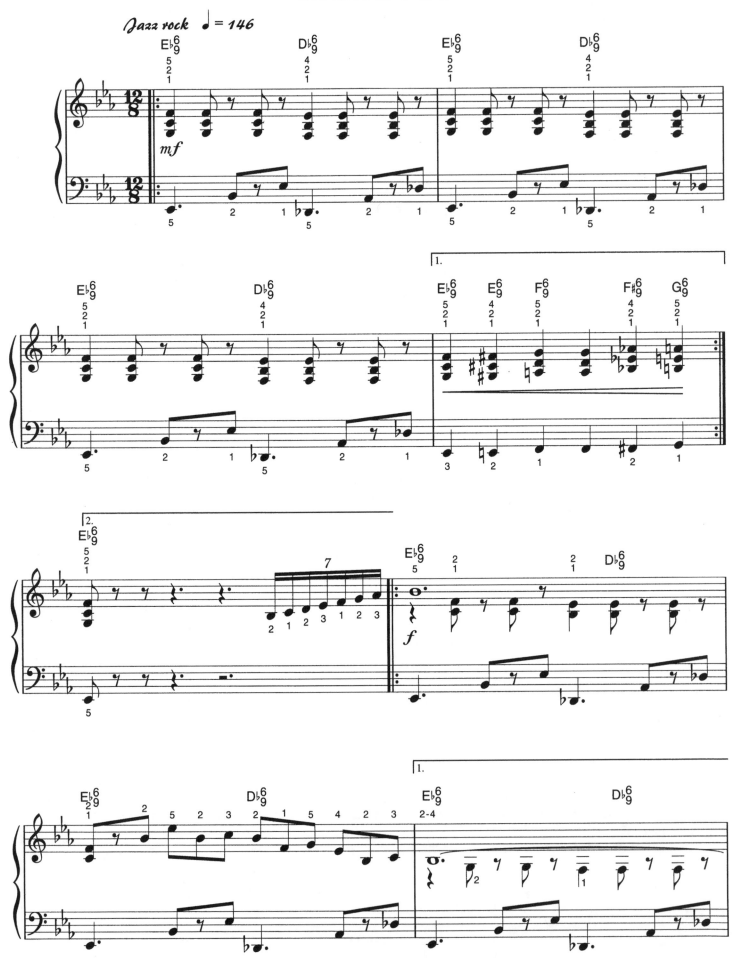

ETUDE #81

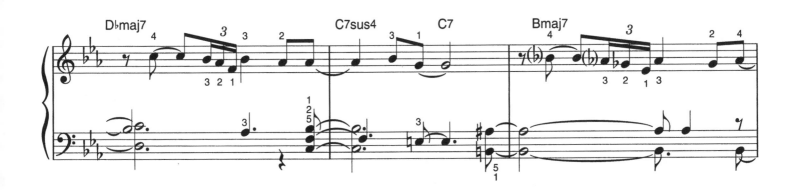

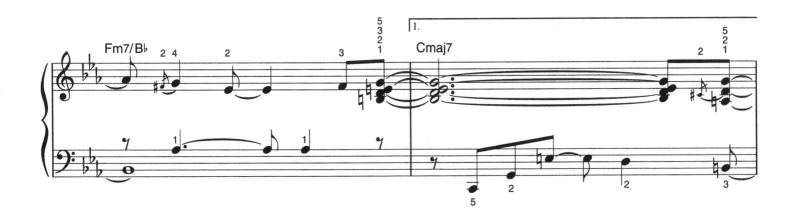

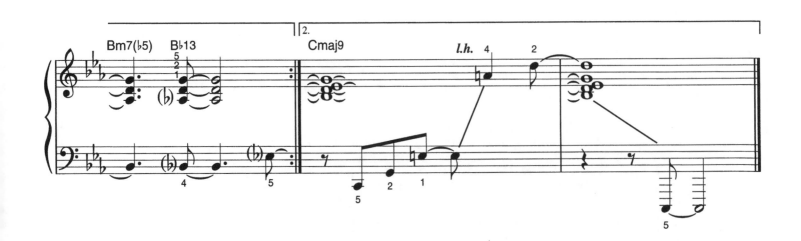

ETUDE #82

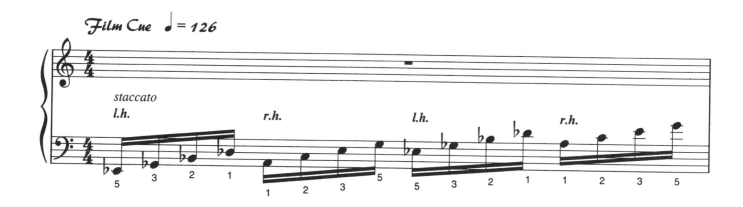

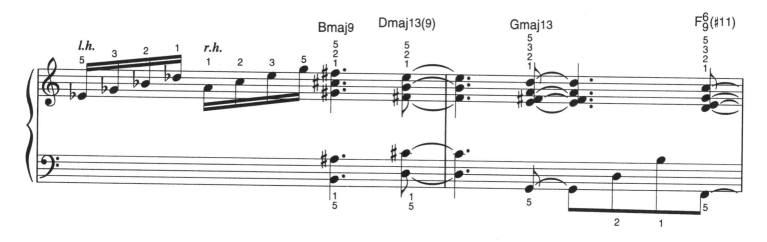

ETUDE #83

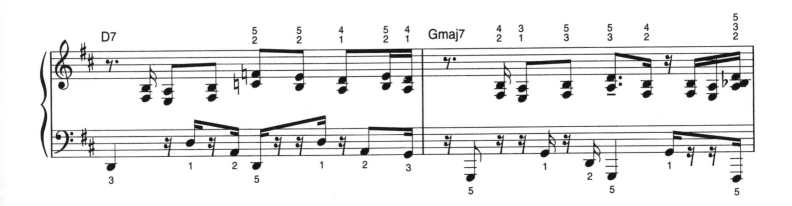

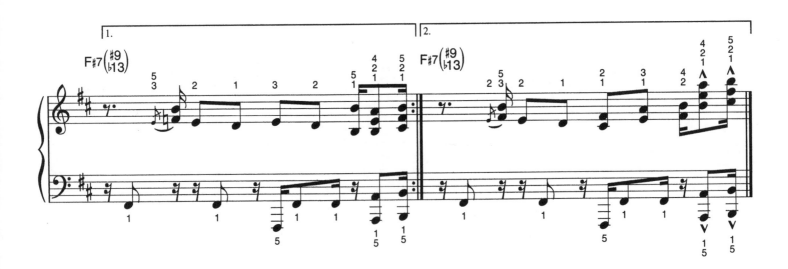

ETUDE #84

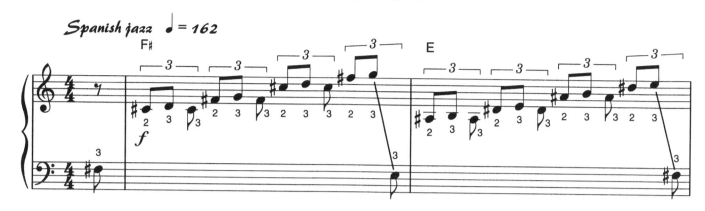

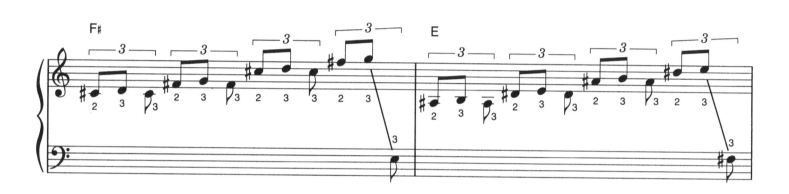

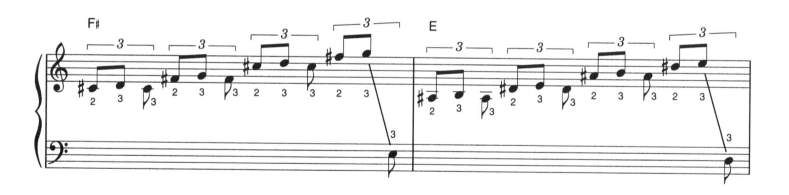

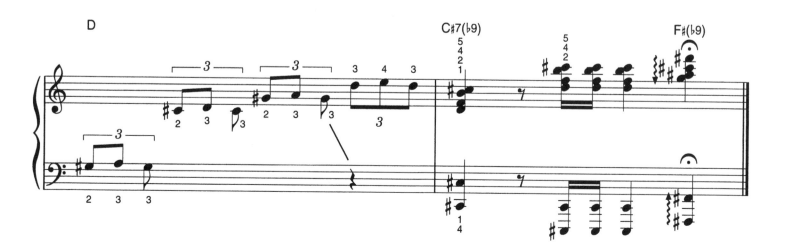

ETUDE #85

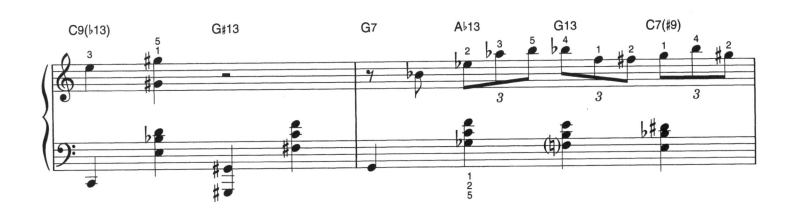

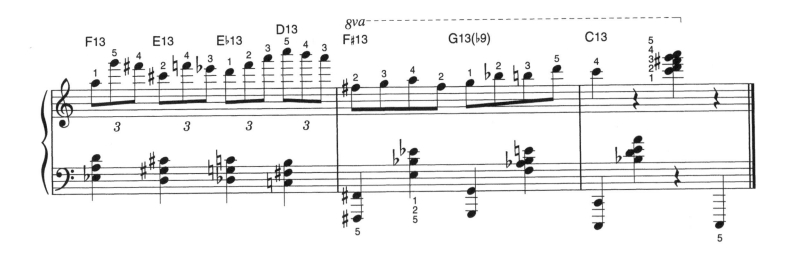

ETUDE #86

The Contemporary Keyboardist™ Stylistic Etude Summaries

Etude #1

Style: R&B Gospel

Musicianship:
1. Key of C, 6/8 gospel feel
2. I-VI-II-V chord progression
3. Two handed octaves
4. Interval playing in the right hand
4. Grace notes

Author's notes: Many many tunes have been written from this simple progression so it would be a good idea to transpose this etude to all keys. Make sure you really duplicate the 6/8 gospel feel on the tape.

Etude #2

Style: Pop Rock Ballad

Musicianship:
1. Key of B flat, 4/4 time
2. I-VI-IV-V progression
3. Hand over hand overlapping arpeggios
4. Triplet rhythm
5. Pedaling

Author's Notes: It's important to really play the overlapping arpeggios smoothlessly while keeping an even triplet rhythm.

Etude #3

Style: Pop Ballad

Musicianship:
1. Key of C, 4/4 time
2. Use of open triads
3. Use of inversions
4. Melodic and rhythmic variations on repeat of theme (measures 6-9)
5. Use of pedal tone on end.
6. Grace notes

Author's Notes: This etude is a great example of how open triads and inversions can be used to create a very modern sound. Should be learned in all keys for sure!

Etude#4

Style: Latin Rock

Musicianship:
1. Key of E flat, 4/4 time
2. Use of tie and syncopation's to create a latin rock sound
3. Use of tenths between hands

Author's Notes: This little common progression with its use of two handed tenths and the common E flat note in the right hand is a good exercise to learn on all keys.

Etude#5

Style: Medium Blues Swing

Musicianship:
1. Key of C-minor, 4/4 time
2. I-bVII-bVI-V progression
3. Swing feel eight notes
4. Use of altered dominant 7th chord (G7#5 and G7#9b13)
5. Left hand bass
6. Use of downward chordal arpeggio in measure #8

Author's Notes: I suggest that once you learn this etude that you try and improvise over the simple bass line C- Bb-Ab-G.

Etude #6

Style: Slow Pop Ballad

Musicianship:
1. Key of C, 4/4 time
2. Extended open voicings (maj9ths and min9ths)
3. Pedaling
4. Grace notes
5. Melody with left hand bass and accompanying figures

Author's notes: This piece should be played differently each time with a lot of expression being careful to bring out the melody. The use of the pedal is important in bringing out the sonorous harmony.

Etude#7

Style: Jazz/Rock

Musicianship:
1. 4/4 time with descending key modulations(G min-F min-Eb min)
2. Use of extended voicings Min9ths and #9ths
3. Left hand broken octaves for bass
4. Grace notes
5. Hand independence because of right hand syncopation's against left hand quarter notes.

Author's Notes:

This is a good example of a common minor progression(I min- b VI Maj7-V7sus). It should actually be transposed down in whole steps until the original starting key of G min is reached.

Etude#8

Style: New Age

Musicianship:
1. Key of E flat, 4/4 time
2. E flat pentatonic scale
3. Melody with left hand arpeggio accompaniment
4. Counterpoint
5. Pedaling

Author's Notes: This is a good piece for playing two handed one line arpeggios and then transferring the arpeggios to the left hand while the right hand assumes the role of playing the melody. It's important to use the pedal to create rich overtones from the E flat major pentatonic scale.

Etude #9

Style: Rock

Musicianship:
1. Key of F Maj, 4/4 time
2. Right hand chordal passage work
3. Accents on beats 2 & 4 and on the & of 4 to create stylistic feel
4. Use of inversions and pedal playing

Author's Notes: Make sure you practice accenting beats 2 and 4 in both hands to create the correct feel. I would practice this etude in all keys as the right hand chordal passage is quite frequently used.

Etude #10

Style: Medium swing

Musicianship:
1. Key of C, 4/4 time
2. Use of dom7th chords and their respective guide tones.
3. Use of dom7th flat 5 substitutes
4. Interval of the tritone (# 4) in right hand

Author's Notes: This etude demonstrates the perfect circle of 5ths in dom7th chords and the use of dom7th flat 5 substitutes. Try also inverting the tritone intervals.

Etude #11

Style: Pop/Rock

Musicianship:
1. Key of C min, 4/4 time
2. Even 8th note right hand chordal passage with chord anticipation's on the & of 4.
3. Left hand bass independence
4. Use of pentatonic scale on Db maj7th chord
5. Use of I-VI-bVI-II-7b5-V7 progression

Aurthor's Notes: This etude serves to teach chord anticipation and right hand left hand independence.

Etude#12

Style: Progressive Pop

Musicianship:
1. Key of C, 4/4 time
2. Hands crossed
3. Use of sus4 and sus 2 chords
4. Hand independence where right hand plays melody while left hand plays steady chords.
5. Grace notes

Author's Notes: This is a good etude demonstrating how the right hand can cross over the left and play a melody in the bass while the left hand comps. Of course, you could also try playing this with the right hand playing the chords and the left hand playing the melody which may even be harder for some independencewise.

Etude#13

Style: New Age Jazz Ballad

Musicianship:
1. Key of C, 4/4 free time
2. Use of bitonality and tensions.
3. Use of upward and downward chordal arpeggios
4. Use of quarter note triplet theme
5. I-IV progression with deceptive resolution III major 7th chord last measure.

Author's Notes: This etude should be played freely paying special attention to bring out the melody and allow the changes to ring. Note the generous use of tensions and how they add color to a simple progression.

Etude #14

Style: Classical Blues

Musicianship
1. Key of C min, cut time
2. Right hand fourths
3. Use of fast alternating hands with C pedal reiterations

Author's Notes: This style of alternating hands is a nice effect on keyboards that everybody should master. Start real slow making sure you play very even and then gradually get faster and faster. Your arms and wrists must stay very relaxed. Once you master this etude, try improvising or writing your own patterns. I suggest you do this in several keys.

Etude #15

Style: Movie Theme Pop Ballad

Musicianship:
1. Key of G Maj, 4/4 free time
2. Use of hybrid chord(no 3rd) and inversions
3. Grace notes
4. Upward and downward arpeggios, both hands.
5. Use of tensions

6. Reading of high treble clef ledger lines.
7. Use of seconds in chord voicings.

Author's Notes: The melody is extremely important in this etude. Experiment with the liberal use of the pedal to create sonorous harmonic effects.

Etude#16

Style: New Age Ballad

Musicianship:
1. Key of C min, 4/4 free time
2. Alternating hand arpeggios
3. I min - IV min progression
4. Large interval skips in arpeggios

Author's Notes: This etude teaches you the use of alternating hands especially when it comes to large interval leaps. Take any chord progression and try improvising or writing one yourself.

Etude#17

Style: Pop Ballad

Musicianship:
1. Key of C Maj, 4/4 time
2. Use of open spread voicings and inversions
3. Descending bass line
4. Use of IV min 7- bVII7(basic II-V) modulating back to C maj.
5. Grace notes

Author's Notes: Again, the melody is extremely important here as it binds the piece together. Sing the melody out loud as you play it to feel the phrasing.

Etude#18

Style: Reggae

Musicianship:
1. Key of C min, 4/4 time
2. Broken octave left hand reggae feel with right hand guitarlike comping triads
3. Use of alternating hand triplets measures 4 & 8.
4. I min-V min-IV min bVI maj-bVII maj - I maj progression

Author's Notes: The triplet or 12/8 like feel is very important to the sound of this etude. Play the piano very percussively, like a drummer, and you'll do fine.

Etude#19

Style: New Age

Musicianship:
1. Key of C, 4/4 free time
2. Alternating hand arpeggios
3. Pedaling
4. High and low ledger line reading

Author's Notes: This etude trains you in fast alternating hand arpeggios with a target melody note at the end both in the treble and then in the bass. It's a nice effect which can be used in a variety of musical situations. This should at least be transposed up a step to D flat to get black key practice.

Etude #20

Style: Jazz Waltz

Musicianship:
1. Key of C Maj, 3/4 waltz time
2. Use of inversions
3. Grace notes
4. Upward and downward arpeggios
5. Left hand bass and right hand melody
6. Low bass ledger line reading

Author's Notes: This is a common jazz waltz feel with a touch of gospel. Once learned you should try and improvise your own melodies over the chord changes. Make sure since this is a jazz feel that your eighth notes are swing feel.

Etude #21

Style: Film Score Cue

Musicianship:
1. Key of G Maj, 4/4 time
2. Right hand augmented chords in whole steps
3. Right hand fourths
4. Left hand rolled octaves

Author's Notes: This usage of augmented chords and chords in fourths is very common. Make sure you play them as legato as possible.

Etude #22

Style: Power Rock

Musicianship:
1. Key of C maj, 4/4 time
2. Use of major chords doubled at the octave without the third for power chord effect
3. Changing time signatures 4/4 to 3/4.

Author's Notes: This etude should be played with a lot of power. Notice how more powerful these chords are without the third present.

Etude#23

Style: Power Rock

Musicianship:
1. C Dorian, 5/4 time
2. Chordal fourths over single note bass line for independence
3. Left hand power octaves(root -fifth-octave)

Author's Notes: This etude demonstrates rock piano in 5/4 time. Should be transposed to all keys to get octave and fourth practice.

Etude#24

Style: Dance Rock Disco

Musicianship:
1. Key of C min, 4/4 time
2. Left hand broken octaves
3. Right hand triad passages
4. Hand independence between octaves and triad passages

Author's Notes: This etude is good for hand independence. Practice the left hand broken octaves first and then slowly add the right triads until you achieve the tempo and independence. If someone can dance to your playing then you've done it!

Etude#25

Style: Medium Swing Modal Jazz

Musicianship:
1. Key of Eb Dorian, 4/4 swing time
2. Left hand Dorian comping in fourths
3. Right hand Dorian melody
4. Fast right hand ending arpeggio
5. Pedaling

Author's Notes: You should extend this etude by improvising in Eb Dorian while comping. This etude should definitely be transposed to all keys.

Etude #26

Style: Progressive Rock

Musicianship:
1. Key of C Maj, 4/4 time
2. Right hand ostinato(repeated figure)
3. Left hand basic melody
4. Pedaling

Author's Notes: Practice the right hand until even and up to speed. Then add the left hand melody making certain that the right hand does not drown it out. Use the pedal to get all the harmonics sounding.

Etude #27

Style: Country Jazz Gospel

Musicianship:
1. Key of C Maj, 4/4 time
2. Left hand um-chuck stride
3. Right hand jazz feel with grace notes, sixth and octaves.
4. Use of inversions and diminished 7th chords.

Author's Notes: Although this style sounds easy, it's quite tricky. Practice the left hand first until perfected and then slowly add the right hand. I would highly advise memorizing this etude so you don't have to watch the score.

Etude#28

Style: Latin

Musicianship:
1. Key of C maj, 4/4 latin time
2. Hand independence and syncopation's
3. Use of II-V I-IV VII-III-VI-II V progression
4. Right Hand Latin figure over characteristic Latin bass line.

Author's Notes: This is initially a very difficult etude due to its rhythmic independence. You must use a metronome or drum machine to keep your time honest until you feel the pocket. Once you hear it though and can play it, it will be very rewarding.

Etude#29

Style: Latin

Musicianship:
1. Key of C maj, 4/4 latin time
2. Latin rhythm syncopations based off of the II-V-I progression
3. Octaves between hands with brief harmony passage at the end.

Authors' Notes: Unlike etude # 28, the rhythmic independence between hands is much simpler. Once you master the syncopation on beat four of each measure, then you have it.

Etude # 30

Style: Latin

Musicianship:
1. Key of C Maj, 4/4 Latin time
2. Rhythmic independence between hands
3. II-7-V7 progression in descending whole steps
4. Right hand octave/third alternations over characteristic Latin bass line.

Author's Notes: Learn each hand separately making sure you play to a metronome. The key to learning this etude is mastering beat four of each measure where the syncopation occurs. You

should transpose this etude to all keys.
Etude #31

Style: Medium Swing Blues

Musicianship:
     1. Key of F min, 4/4 swing time
     2. Two handed octave playing
     3. Two handed spread voicings measures 11-14.
     4. Minor blues progression
     5. Grace notes

Author's Notes: Make sure you really lock the octaves together so they sound as one line. I would transpose this to all keys or at least the common blues keys of Cmin, Emin, Amin, Gmin, Dmin and Bbmin.

Etude#32

Style: Latin

Musicianship:
     1. Key of C min, cut time
     2. Two hand octave lines branching into harmony
     3. Cut time(2/2) Latin feel.
     4. Use of the Dom7th #9 chord.

Author's Notes: Make sure you feel the cut time meaning two pulses per measure. Use a metronome or drum machine and also make sure your eighth note syncopations are accurate.

Etude #33

Style: Modal Jazz

Musicianship:
     1. Key of G Phrygian
     2. Changing time signatures
     3. Two part playing- left hand bass, right hand melody.
     4. Grace notes

Author's Notes: Demonstrates accents in phrasing due to changing time signatures.

Etude #34

Style: Classical

Musicianship:
1. Key of F Min, 4/4 time
2. Alternating hand octave reiterations
3. Right hand arpeggio in fourths

Author's Notes: Practice very slowly and memorize the pattor. Then gradually and very accurately speed it up to the indicated tempo and beyond. Your wrist and arm must relax in order to get the appropriate bounce and muscle control.

Etude#35

Style Gospel Rock

Musicianship:
1. Key of C maj, 4/4 time
2. bVII-IV-I progression
3. Grace notes
4. 32nd note fills
5. Octave passages in right hand

Author's Notes: This etude is reminiscent of Elton John's style. It has many syncopated rhythms between the left and right hand and is more difficult to read than play once you hear and feel it. Definitely practice hands separately at first.

Etude#36

Style: Blues/Rock

Musicianship:
1. Key of G Maj, 4/4 time
2. Use of major chord without 3rds for power chords.
3. Use of Blues scales
4. Fourth passage in right hand

Author's notes: This etude simulates power blues rock and blends nicely with guitar players. The chords should be played loud with a strong attack. I would learn this in all keys if you want to pursue this style further.

Etude #37

Style: Progressive Rock

Musicianship:
1. Key of D min, 4/4 time
2. Use of two part counterpoint in right hand
3. Grace notes
4. Broken left hand octaves
5. 16th note sus chord passages.

Author's Notes: This etude relies on a good stable and strong left hand. Once you get that going, work on the right hand counterpoint making sure you really bring out the parts.

Etude#38

Style: Soul/R&B

Musicianship:
1. Key of B Flat, 4/4 time
2. Use of dominant 7th guide tones with half step approaches
3. Left hand bass
4. Spread dominant 13th voicings last two measures
5. Use of tension #11 in last Bb713#11 voicing.

Author's Notes: The right hand of this etude simulates the horn section of the old R&B/Soul era. Make sure you use the indicated fingering so you play a good legato.

Etude #39

Style: R & B

Musicianship:
1. Key of C, 4/4 time
2. Left hand bass, right hand horn punches with syncopations on the and of beat 4.
3. Grace notes
4. Spread dominant 13th voicings last few measures
5. Hand independence between bass and chord punches
6. Basic use of I-IV-V progression with bVII-V-IV-bIII tag.

Author's Notes: Listen to the feel of the recording making sure you really create a good dance pocket with a lot of dynamics and feeling. It would be good to learn this in all keys.

Etude #40

Style: Modal Jazz

Musicianship:
1. Key of C Maj, 4/4 swing time
2. Use of parallel dominant 7 sus chords.
3. Swing eighths
4. Melody based on interconnecting dom7th scales(mixolydian scale)
5. Chord progression based on C natural minor scale(Aeolian)
6. Left hand comping in fourths

Author's Notes: This is a good example of creating a melody over one type chord progression - in this case Dom7 sus chords. After you learn it, definitely practice improvising and creating your own melodies over these changes.

Etude#41

Style: Blocked Chord Swing

Musicianship:
1. Key of C maj, 4/4 swing time
2. Use of blocked chord(doubled melody in the base with chord) style.
3. Grace notes
4. Use of two handed tenths in measure 9.

Author's Notes: This style sounds great on keyboards and simulates horn section playing. Definitely should be learned in all keys. Also suggest listening to George Shearing and Oscar Peterson.

Etude #42

Style: Avant Garde

Musianship:
1. Key of B in the non traditional sense, 4/4 free time
2. Hand cluster in left hand
3. Alternating hand clusters
4. Bitonality - C over B
5. Dissonance
6. Pedaling and overlapping tonal centers

Author's Notes: The world of the avant garde is quite fun to research and experiment with as it opens up your ears to new possibilities. Experiment with trying to make this etude your own. Really try and prehear these new type sounds and play them with conviction. Then for real fun, improvise and write your own in this style still trying of course to be as musical as possible.

Etude#43

Style: Funk

Musicianship:
1. Key of D min, 4/4 16th note feel time
2. Syncopated left hand bass
3. Right hand triadic 16th note feel chordal passages
4. Grace notes
5. D blues scale in measures 4 & 8.
6. Funk clavinet type alternating hand independence

Author's Notes: This is one of my favorite type styles and unfortunately it can be a difficult one to learn. Although you can practice this hands separately, I find it best to practice hands together immediately taking each beat and slowing it down until you line up each hand's function. Since this style is predominantly based on a subdivision of 4(16th notes), doing it in this manner will keep this subdivision intact and make your task easier. Good luck!

Etude #44

Style: Progressive Rock

Musicianship:

1. Key of C min, 4/4 time
2. Hand independence with accented 16th notes over steady quarter notes
3. Continuous right hand 16th note phrase

Author's Notes: This etude shows the importance of correct fingering in order to play this continuous 16th note passage. It also teaches the effect of accents - measure 1 - where the 16th notes are divided into a phrase of 3+3+3+3+4. My suggestion is to learn the piece first without the accents and then later add them very slowly until you feel them.

Etude #45

Style: Contemporary Jazz Ballad

Musicianship:
1. Key of Eb Maj, 4/4 free time
2. Use of spread voicings, clusters and tensions.
3. Use of chord tremolo in last measure
4. Extended grace note approach in left hand measure 3.

Author's Notes: This etude demonstrates a thick complex but flowing harmony and is representative of contemporary solo jazz piano. Don't allow the rich harmonies to distract you from bringing out the melody.

Etude #46

Style: Jazz/Funk

Musicianship:
1. Key of D Min
2. Use of short duration syncopated chord punches
3. Two part counterpoint in right hand measure 2
4. Use of triads superimposed over bass notes.

Author's Notes: In order to correctly play this piece, you must accurately sense the 16th note subdivision. Practice with a metronome and hands separately and play along with the recording as much as possible.

Etude #47

Style: Blues

Musicianship:
1. Key of C Maj, 6/4 time
2. Left hand ascending maj seconds
3. Right hand blues scale
4. Reading of low ledger notes in the bass
5. Grace notes
6. Independence between hands - syncopated melody over continuous eighth notes

Author's Notes: This is an interesting 6/4 blues that demands playing a blues melody over a continuous unusual ascending major second passage. Definitely practice hands separately first on this on being careful to really work the fingering and aligning the left and right hands up.

Etude #48

Style: Gospel

Musicianship:
1. Key of C Maj, 4/4 free time
2. Use of dim7th chord and inversions
3. Chord tremolos
4. Use of blues scale and idiomatic gospel licks

Author's Notes: The #II passing diminished 7th chord to the I chord in first inversion(D#dim7th - C7/E) is a real characteristic gospel sounding progression. Add the chord tremolos, blues/gospel licks and Amen!

Etude#49

Style: Pop

Musicianship:
1. Key of C maj, 4/4 time
2. I-VI-IV-V progression
3. Grace notes
4. Left hand steady bass, right hand repeating chord voicing.
5. Hand independence - syncopated chords against quarter notes

Author's Notes: Just make sure you play to a metronome so you don't speed up which is the tendency on this etude.

Etude#50

Style: Latin

Musicianship:
1. Key of C min, 4/4Latin time
2. Left hand bass, right hand Latin syncopated chords
3. Use of descending cliché line progression I min-I minmaj7-I min7 - I min6
4. Use of Vsusb9 chord measure 11.
5. Two hand octaves measure 12.

Author's Notes: This etude demonstrates the cliche line based on the variation of the min chord. I would learn this therefore in all keys. Notice how the Latin rhythmic figure was kept up through the whole piece, even on the maj 7 and G sus chords at the end.

Etude#51

Style: Gospel

Musicianship:
1. Key of C maj, 3/4 time
2. Grace notes
3. Descending bass lines due to use of inversions
4. Use of 16th note 5 groupings
5. Use of triplet feel

Author's Notes: This 3/4 gospel feel with left hand octaves and syncopations should really give you a taste of this emotional style. A must in all keys for best and lasting results.

Etude #52

Style:Jazz/Gospel

Musicianship:
1. Key of Eb maj, 4/4 time
2. Complex rhythmic independence between hands
3. Group of eight 32nd notes measure 16
4. Parallel arpeggios in harmony last measure

Author's Notes: This etude must be practiced hands separately at first and then slowly put together. Once learned, this style is very useful as it combines gospel and jazz harmony with complex 16th subdivision variations. The melody should really sing.

Etude#53

Style: Jazz blues

Musicianship:
1. Key of C maj, 4/4 time
2. Jazz blues harmony with bebop type jazz melody
3. Left hand comp chords
4. Hand independence
5. Swing feel
6. Fast right hand ending cadenza fill last three measures.

Author's Notes: This is referred to in my book. The Contemporary Keyboardist™ as Blues form #2 - jazz blues. Definitely learn hands separately. Once learned, transpose to all keys. Rather than just playing blues licks, this melody outlines the changes and is a good example of bebop type blowing.

Etude#54

Style: Stride jazz

Musicianship:
1. Key of C maj, 4/4 time
2. Left hand um chuck stride (alternating bass and chord voicing)
3. Descending dominant 7th chords with tensions
4. Grace notes
5. Fast two hand octave Dom7 cadenza measure 8.
6. Low bass and treble clef notation

Author's Notes: Definitely learn the left hand first to develop this left hand dexterity. Once the melody is learned, put both hands together very slowly experimenting with the use of the pedal. Then try improvising and writing melodies yourself over the changes.

Etude#55

Style: Fast Bebop

Musicianship:
1. Key of C maj, 4/4 time
2. Left hand walking bass with right hand fast swing bebop 16th notes
3. Fast line fingering concepts
4. Line writing over descending dom7th chords.

Author's Notes: This is a good etude to gain experience on soloing over dom7th chords and as well experience on the type of fingering necessary to play fast jazz lines.

Etude#56

Style: Jazz Swing

Musicianship:
1. Key of C maj, 4/4 time
2. Left hand shell voicings(root-7, 3-7 etc)
3. Chromatic approach chord(Db69 to C maj7) last measure
4. Right hand bebop jazz lines
5. I(III)-VI-II-V type progression soloing.

Author's Notes: This an example of how simple left hand shell type voicings can support a right hand jazz solo. This would be a good etude to transpose to all keys in order to get not only left hand voicing practice but also practice in bebop lines in all keys.

Etude #57

Style: Avant Garde

Musicianship:
1. C tonality, 2/4 time
2. Two hand alternating clusters(seconds)
3. Minor second dissonant melody last measure.

Author's Notes: This etude should give you many ideas as to how to play percussive shapes on the piano which after all is a percussive instrument as well as a melodic one.

Etude#58

Style: Classical Pop

Musicianship:
1. Key of C min, 4/4 time
2. VIIdim - I progression
3. Inversions
4. Grace notes
5. Fast right hand arpeggio last measure

Author's Notes: This is almost a modern day chorale(4 part writing of the baroque era). Once learned, study the harmony and notice the temporary modulations and then the switch to C major at the end.

Etude#59

Style: Progressive Rock Fusion

Musicianship:
1. Key of C min., 4/4 time
2. Alternating hand percussive figures
3. Based primarily on C blues sale
4. Use of circle of fifths last 4 measures

Author's Notes: Practice very slowly with both hands together until your arms and wrists get the appropriate bounce to accurately get up to tempo.

Etude#60

Style: Progressive Rock

Musicianship:
1. Key of C min, 6/8 time
2. Left hand crossing over the right.
3. 16th note phrase with accents
4. Circle of fifths measures 7-9.
5. Pedaling

Author's Notes: This is a fun percussive study demonstrating how the left hand can play bass and also then cross over the right to play a melody note. Use the pedal to get everything ringing.

Etude#61

Style: Swing

Musicianship:
1. Key of C maj, 4/4 time
2. Left hand melodic playing
3. Use of pedal and descending fifths

Author's Notes: This is simply an example of playing through a progression with just the left hand

When playing left hand only studies, fingering can be very important.
Etude#62

Style: Progressive Rock

Musicianship:
1. Key of G min, 7/4
2. Independence between hands
3. Right hand melodic playing in 7/4 over ostinato left hand figure.
4. Right hand arpeggio in last measure

Author's Notes: This can be a tricky etude because of trying to get used to 7/4 on a 4/4 planet! Practice slowly and with caution or you'll end up in 4/4. Definately use a metronome or drum machine.

Etude #63

Style: Shuffle Funk

Musicianship:
1. Key of E min , 4/4 time
2. Alternating hand playing
3. E blues scale riff measure 6
4. Deceptive resolution to F69 last measure

Author's Notes: This alternating hands style playing is very useful and should be practiced slowly keeping the shuffle feel indicated. Then try improvising yourself in E minor with similar ideas.

Etude #64

Style: Power Rock

Musicianship:
1. Key of E min, 4/4 time
2. Power chords(octave and fifths with no thirds)
3. Inversions

Author's Notes: This rock style is accomplished with the use of octaves and fifths with no thirds. Use a lot of arm to produce a powerful tone. Suggest you feel the subdivision of even eighth notes to keep the correct pocket feel.

Etude #65

Style: Gospel Pop

Musicianship:
1. Key of Bb, 3/4 time
2. Use of continuous chord tremolos for gospel effect
3. Chord and bass accompaniment on B section measures 9-16.
4. Inversions

Author's Notes: This study will require some muscle endurance and vice versa, this study, if practiced daily, will increase your muscle stamina which is necessary to perform continuous tremolos.

Tremolo technique is a combination of finger and slight arm rotation. Good luck!
Etude #66

Style: Chicago Rock

Musicianship:
1. Key of Bb min, 4/4 time
2. Chord comping with bass accompaniment.
3. Syncopated chord pushes on the & of 4.
4. Use of standard II-V progression.

Author's Notes: Practice separately at first to a metronome and then, when putting it together, make sure that the chord pushes don't cause you to rush the time.

Etude#67

Style: Pop/Rock

Musicianship:
1. Key of G min, alternating 7/8 and 4/4.
2. Sustained chords with left hand bass
3. Two hand octaves with fourth intervals for power
4. Two hand tremolo last measure

Author's Notes: This etude teaches alternating time feels. It also demonstrates sustained chords in the right hand while left hand takes the bass player role which happens a lot when playing split or multi-keyboards.

Etude#68

Style: Blues

Musicianship:
1. Key of G Maj, 4/4 time
2. Right hand trills alternating between 16ths and triplets
3. Left hand bass and shell voicings

Author's Notes: Although this is just a simple blues, it also is a continuous trill study. I would practice the trill separately until I mastered its fingering and endurance problems and then add the left hand. Be careful of the 16th to triplet transition and back!

Etude#69

Style: Contemporary Jazz Ballad

Musicianship:
1. Key of F maj, 4/4 free time
2. Use of complex spread and extended voicings
3. Counterpoint
4. Hand over hand arpeggios
5. Grace notes

Etude #70

Style: Shuffle Blues

Musicianship:
    1. Key of C Maj, 4/4 time
    2. Triplet shuffle feel
    3. Hand independence
    4. Tremolos
    5. Grace notes
    6. Groups of six 16th notes measures 7-10.
    7. Blues cadenza ad lib.

Author's Notes: This style sounds simple but can be very complex due to it's hand independence difficulties. A definite hands separate at first practice. Suggest transposing to other commonly played blues keys like F, Bb, G, & E.

Etude#71

Style: Boogie Woogie

Musicianship:
    1. Key of C maj, 4/4 time
    2. Left hand boogie woogie broken octave pattern
    3. Right hand chord punctuations
    4. Simple three chord(I-IV-V) blues pattern

Author's Notes: This is a good etude to get practice at playing broken octave boogie woogie. Accuracy is the challenge here as well as endurance. Play extremely slow until your accuracy improves and then add the right hand and gradually speed up. Patience is a virtue!

Etude#72

Style: Jazz Swing

Musicianship:
    1. Key of C maj, 4/4 time
    2. Left hand walking bass with right hand melody.
    3. Fast 16th note right hand jazz lines

Author's Notes: This dominant 7th I-VI-II-V progression is yet another example of left hand walking bass with right hand blowing. The 16th note phrases will help you learn fingering concepts for playing these type of fast jazz lines.

Etude#73

Style: Fast Swing

Musicianship:
      1. Key of C Maj, 4/4 time
      2. Fast right hand chromatic jazz lines
      3. Two handed fast parallel arpeggios last measure

Author's Notes: In playing fast chromatic-type jazz lines, fingering, besides of course hearing, can be a major hurdle. This short etude will give you some nice fingering concepts. Try improvising chromatic lines yourself once you think you got the hang of it.

Etude#74

Style: Swing Blues

Musicianship:
      1. Key of G maj, 4/4 time
      2. Use of dom7th left hand fourth voicings
      3. Sym dim half/whole scales measures 4, 10, 12, and 15.

Author's Notes: This is just a three chord blues in G that features dom7th left hand comping ideas. Should be learned in all keys. Try improvising over these voicings yourself.

Etude#75

Style: New Age Modal

Musicianship:
      1. Key of Eb dorian(D flat), 7/8 time
      2. Left hand ostinato(repetitive figure) with right hand melody
      3. Hand independence.
      4. Clef changes
      5. Hand over hand arpeggio last measure.
      6. Fourth right hand chordal passages

Author's Notes: Learn and memorize the left hand ostinato and then add the right hand melody at a slow tempo. Once you get it fast, you'll just hear the flow but have patience as this may take some time as you have to also get used to the 7/8 time signature.

Etude#76

Style: Jazz Ballad

Musicianship:
1. Key of C maj, 4/4 free time
2. Fast pentatonic and diatonic approach passages
3. Modal interchange on final chord(C69 to C minmaj7
4. Use of parallel Dom7 13 chords in descending minor 3rds
5. Left hand fourth comp voicings
6. Right hand fast arpeggio

Author's Notes: This etude has a variety of fundamentals built into it. As always, the melody is the most important concern. Suggest you practice all scale fingerings on the fast passages as they are very important.

Etude#77

Style: Progressive Rock

Musicianship:
1. C min, 4/4 time
2. Accented 16th notes
3. Hand independence
4. Left hand syncopations
5. Left hand octaves

Author's Notes: This is a good study in right hand accented 16th notes over a syncopated bass line. It also shows a contemporary use of right hand triads over various bass roots.

Etude#78

Style: Progressive Pop/Rock

Musicianship:
1. Key of C maj, 4/4 time
2. Voice led chords with inversions
3. Hand independence
4. Octave bass line
5. Cadenza ad lib on ending major 7 chord.

Author's Notes: This is a very tight voice led little study demonstrating left hand bass lines and right hand voicings that lead smoothly to each other. Be careful not to rush the time with all the chord pushes. Feel free to make your own cadenza ad lib at the end if you like.

Etude #79

Style: New Age

Musicianship:
      1. Key of Eb maj, 4/4 time
      2. Hand independence - melody over ostinato left hand
      3. Tremolos
      4. Time signature changes

Author's Notes: This is a beautifully flowing etude once you get the left hand rolling. Use the pedal to keep the sounds interacting and by all means make the melody sing.

Etude#80

Style: Jazz/Rock

Musicianship:
      1. Key of Eb, 12/8 time
      2. Hand independence
      3. Two part right hand playing
      4. Right hand fourth voicings
      5. Rhythmic grouping of 7

Author's Notes: This is a very common 12/8 type feel that demands a good sense of time and hand independence to keep it all on track. Although you can practice hands together, I find it better to practice hands together pretty quickly but very slow at first so you can hear the correct feel right from the beginning.

Etude#81

Style: Jazz Swing

Musicianship:
      1. Key of Eb maj, 4/4 time
      2. Hand independence
      3. Grace notes
      4. Inversions
      5. Deceptive resolution to VI major7 chord(C maj7)
      6. Left hand shell voicings and bass playing

Author's Notes: This short study demonstrates a descending progression over which a right hand melody floats. Definitely practice hands separately first and then the independence problems won't be so difficult.

Etude#82

Style: Film Cue

Musicianship:
   1. Key of E maj, 4/4 time
   2. Alternating hand tritone stacatto arpeggios
   3. Parallel major 7 type voicings
   4. Right hand arpeggio last two measures

Author's Notes: The use of min7 tetrads a tritone a part (aug 4th) create an interesting dark effect. Use a slight wrist or arm staccato for the arpeggios and then a smooth legato for the major 7th chords.

Etude #83

Style: Slow Funk

Musicianship:
   1. Key of B min, 4/4 time
   2. Hand independence
   3. Fourth intervals over single note bass lines
   4. Imin7-bIII7-bVI Maj7-V7 progression

Author's Notes: The interaction between hands is very tricky in this study. You must keep a steady pulse and hear the 16th note subdivisions to execute this etude. Listen to the recording a lot.

Etude#84

Style: Spanish Jazz

Musicianship:
   1. Key of F# Spanish, 4/4 time
   2. Hand over hand patterns
   3. Maj and dominant chords with b9 Spanish sound
   4. Triplet figures

Author's Notes: This etude should be practiced very very slow and even. Once the hands become coordinated, then go for it. Playing a line with alternating hands is an important piano trick.

Etude#85

Style: Dissonant Stride

Musicianship:
1. Key of C maj, 4/4 time
2. Um chuck(bass-chord) stride dom7th chords
3. Angular right hand melody using many tensions and dissonances
4. Staccato left hand with legato right hand
5. Hand independence
6. High treble clef notation

Author's Notes: This um chuck stride etude with a dissonant melody is a lot of fun. Practice the left hand many many times and then add the right. Otherwise, you'll crash and burn! Try improvising your own using random dom 7th voicings.

Etude#86

Style: Atonal

Musicianship:
1. Chromatic key center, 4/4 time
2. Alternating hands
3. Percussive staccato touch
4. Use of seconds, fourths, and clusters

Author's Notes: Practice hands together immediately but very very slow. I would memorize this etude at a slow tempo and then gradually play it faster and faster. Makes a good show off piece at auditions or when you're trying out a new keyboard at a music store.